revise

GCSE

Modern World History

John Patrick

with Tony Buzan

Hodder & Stoughton

A MEMBER OF THE HODDER HEADLINE GROUP

Photographic credits

Imperial War Museum, pp. 10, 17, 93; Centre for the Study of Cartoons and Caricature, University of Kent, Canterbury, pp. 24, 31, 98; *Punch*, pp. 27, 31, 35, 117; Private collection, p.40; David King Collection, p.42; Topham Picturepoint, p.51; Novosti Photo Library, p.53; Corbis-Bettmann/UPI p.64; E.T. Archive, p.82; Peter Newark's Military Pictures, p.90; Bilderdienst Süddeutscher Verlag, pp. 101, 136; Weidenfeld & Nicolson, p.105; Engelhardt in the *St Louis Post-Dispatch*, p.123.

ISBN 0 340 66385 5

First published 1997
Impression number   10 9 8 7 6 5 4 3 2 1
Year   2001 2000 1999 1998 1997

The 'Teach Yourself' name and logo are registered trade marks of Hodder & Stoughton Ltd.

Designed and produced by Gecko Ltd, Bicester, Oxon
Printed in Great Britain for Hodder & Stoughton Educational, a division of Hodder Headline Plc, 338 Euston Road, London NW1 3BH by Scotprint Ltd, Musselburgh, Scotland.

Mind Maps: David Brady, Helen Whitten
Illustrations: Harvey Collins, Andrea Norton, Stephen Ramsay
Cover design: Amanda Hawkes
Cover illustration: Paul Bateman

Contents

Revision made easy

The four pages that follow contain a gold mine of information on how you can achieve success both at school and in your exams. Read them and apply the information, and you will be able to spend less, but more efficient, time studying, with better results. If you already have another *Hodder & Stoughton Revision Guide*, skim-read these pages to remind yourself about the exciting new techniques the books use, then move ahead to page 1.

This section gives you vital information on how to remember more *while* you are learning and how to remember more *after* you have finished studying. It explains

> how to use special techniques to improve your memory

> how to use a revolutionary note-taking technique called Mind Maps that will double your memory and help you to write essays and answer exam questions

> how to read everything faster while at the same time improving your comprehension and concentration

All this information is packed into the next four pages, so make sure you read them!

Your *amazing* memory

There are five important things you must know about your brain and memory to revolutionise your school life.

1 how your memory ('recall') works *while* you are learning

2 how your memory works *after* you have finished learning

3 how to use Mind Maps – a special technique for helping you with all aspects of your studies

4 how to increase your reading speed

5 how to zap your revision

1 Recall during learning – the need for breaks

When you are studying, your memory can concentrate, understand and remember well for between 20 and 45 minutes at a time. Then it *needs* a break. If you carry on for longer than this without one, your memory starts to break down! If you study for hours non-stop, you will remember only a fraction of what you have been trying to learn, and you will have wasted valuable revision time.

So, ideally, *study for less than an hour*, then take a five- to ten-minute break. During the break listen to music, go for a walk, do some exercise, or just daydream. (Daydreaming is a necessary brain-power booster – geniuses do it regularly.) During the break your brain will be sorting out what it has been learning, and you will go back to your books with the new information safely stored and organised in your memory banks. We recommend breaks at regular intervals as you work through the *Revision Guides*. Make sure you take them!

2 Recall after learning – the waves of your memory

What do you think begins to happen to your memory straight *after* you have finished learning something? Does it immediately start forgetting? No! Your brain actually *increases* its power and carries on remembering. For a short time after your study session, your brain integrates the information, making a more complete picture of everything it has just learnt. Only then does the rapid decline in memory begin, and as much as 80 per cent of what you have learnt can be forgotten in a day.

However, if you catch the top of the wave of your memory, and briefly review (look back over) what you have been revising at the correct time, the memory is stamped in far more strongly, and stays at the crest of the wave for a much longer time. To maximise your brain's power to remember, take a few minutes and use a Mind Map to review what you have learnt at the end of a day. Then review it at the end of a week, again at the end of a month, and finally a week before the exams. That way you'll ride your memory wave all the way to your exam – and beyond!

Amazing as your memory is (think of everything you actually do have stored in your brain at this moment) the principles on which it operates are very simple: your brain will remember if it (a) has an image (a picture or a symbol); (b) has that image fixed and (c) can link that image to something else.

3 The Mind Map® – a picture of the way you think

Do you *like* taking notes? More importantly, do you like having to go back over and learn them before exams? Most students I know certainly do not! And how do you take your notes? Most people take notes on lined paper, using blue or black ink. The result, visually, is *boring*! And what does your brain do when it is bored? It turns off, tunes out, and goes to sleep! Add a dash of colour, rhythm, imagination, and the whole note-taking process becomes much more fun, uses more of your brain's abilities, *and* improves your recall and understanding.

A Mind Map mirrors the way your brain works. It can be used for note-taking from books or in class, for reviewing what you have just studied, for revising, and for essay planning for coursework and in exams. It uses all your memory's natural techniques to build up your rapidly growing 'memory muscle'.

You will find Mind Maps throughout this book. Study them, add some colour, personalise them, and then have a go at drawing your own – you'll remember them far better! Put them on your walls and in your files for a quick-and-easy review of the topic.

How to draw a Mind Map

- Start in the middle of the page with the page turned sideways. This gives your brain the maximum room for its thoughts.

- Always start by drawing a small picture or symbol. Why? Because a picture is worth a thousand words to your brain. And try to use at least three colours, as colour helps your memory even more.

- Let your thoughts flow, and write or draw your ideas on coloured branching lines connected to your central image. These key symbols and words are the headings for your topic. The Mind Map at the top of the next page shows you how to start.

- Then add facts and ideas by drawing more, smaller, branches on to the appropriate main branches, just like a tree.

- Always print your word clearly on its line. Use only one word per line. The Mind Map at the foot of the

next page shows you how to do this.

- To link ideas and thoughts on different branches, use arrows, colours, underlining, and boxes.

How to read a Mind Map

- Begin in the centre, the focus of your topic.

- The words/images attached to the centre are like chapter headings, read them next.

- Always read out from the centre, in every direction (even on the left-hand side, where you will have to read from right to left, instead of the usual left to right).

Using Mind Maps

Mind Maps are a versatile tool – use them for taking notes in class or from books, for solving problems, for brainstorming with friends, and for reviewing and revising for exams – their uses are endless! You will find them invaluable for planning essays for coursework and exams. Number your main branches in the order in which you want to use them and off you go – the main headings for your essay are done and all your ideas are logically organised!

4 Super speed reading

It seems incredible, but it's been proved – the faster you read, the more you understand and remember! So here are some tips to help you to practise reading faster – you'll cover the ground more quickly, remember more, *and* have more time for revision!

★ First read the whole text (whether it's a lengthy book or an exam paper) very quickly, to give your brain an overall idea of what's ahead and get it working. (It's like sending out a scout to look at the territory you have to cover – it's much easier when you know what to expect!) Then read the text again for more detailed information.

★ Have the text a reasonable distance away from your eyes. In this way your eye/brain system will be able to see more at a glance, and will naturally begin to read faster.

★ Take in groups of words at a time. Rather than reading 'slowly and carefully' read faster, more enthusiastically. Your comprehension will rocket!

★ Take in phrases rather than single words while you read.

★ Use a guide. Your eyes are designed to follow movement, so a thin pencil underneath the lines you are reading, moved smoothly along, will 'pull' your eyes to faster speeds.

5 Helpful hints for exam revision

Start to revise at the beginning of the course. Cram at the start, not the end and avoid 'exam panic'!

Use Mind Maps throughout your course, and build a Master Mind Map for each subject – a giant Mind Map that summarises everything you know about the subject.

Use memory techniques such as mnemonics (verses or systems for remembering things like dates and events, or lists).

Get together with one or two friends to revise, compare Mind Maps, and discuss topics.

And finally...

⭐ *Have fun while you learn* – studies show that those people who enjoy what they are doing understand and remember it more, and generally do it better.

⭐ *Use your teachers* as resource centres. Ask them for help with specific topics and with more general advice on how you can improve your all-round performance.

⭐ *Personalise your **Revision Guide*** by underlining and highlighting, by adding notes and pictures. Allow your brain to have a conversation with it!

Your brain is an amazing piece of equipment – learn to use it, and you, like thousands of students before you will be able to master 'B's and 'A's with ease. The more you understand and use your brain, the more it will repay you!

TRAIN YOUR BRAIN!

BRAIN TRAINERS

Preface

This book is designed to help you achieve a better grade in GCSE Modern World History.

It doesn't give you every single fact you will need to do well. The syllabuses of the various examination groups all differ, and every syllabus also offers schools some choice in what they study. So only your teacher knows exactly how much you need to cover, and at what depth.

The main aim of this book is to try to help you think about the subject along the lines that GCSE examiners expect.

In doing this, it gives you practice in using sources and in answering the kinds of questions you will meet in GCSE papers, with hints on how to tackle them and with some model answers.

In addition, some of the Mind Maps will remind you of aspects of the various topics which are not dealt with in detail in the text.

I hope you will find the book useful.

John Patrick

Key to symbols

As you read through this revision guide, you will notice symbols which occur frequently throughout the book. These are to help you identify specific sections of text quickly and easily while you revise. This is what they mean:

(a) Notes: drawing your attention to specific sections of text, features on maps or statistics.

(b) Check: end-of-section reviews and revision tips.

Specimen question: questions to answer to help with your revision, based on the section you have just read. These are typical of GCSE exam questions.

Model answer: A guide to what the examiners will expect to read in your answer.

Hint: how to set about answering the question to get the best marks.

Some Milestones in 20th-century History

1905	Russian Revolution
1914	First World War begins
1917	Russian Revolution – Lenin comes to power
1918	First World War ends
1919	Peace treaties signed
	League of Nations established
1922	Mussolini seizes power in Italy
1923	Collapse of the German mark
1924	Death of Lenin – Stalin takes over in USSR
1929	Wall Street Crash
1931	Japan invades Manchuria
1932	Depth of the Great Depression
1933	Hitler takes over in Germany
	Roosevelt becomes President of USA – launches 'New Deal'
1935	Mussolini invades Abyssinia
1937	Civil War breaks out in Spain
1939	Second World War begins
1941	Pearl Harbor – Japan and USA enter war
1945	A bombs dropped on Japan
	Second World War ends
	United Nations Organisation established
1947	India and Pakistan granted independence
1948	Berlin blockade
1949	Mao sets up People's Republic of China
1950	Korean War breaks out
1953	Death of Stalin
1956	Hungarian revolt
1961	Berlin wall built
1962	Cuban Missile Crisis
1965	US troops land in Vietnam
1968	The Prague Spring
1975	US troops leave Vietnam
1980	Rise of Solidarity in Poland
1985	Gorbachev takes over in the USSR
1989	Berlin Wall opened

The First World War

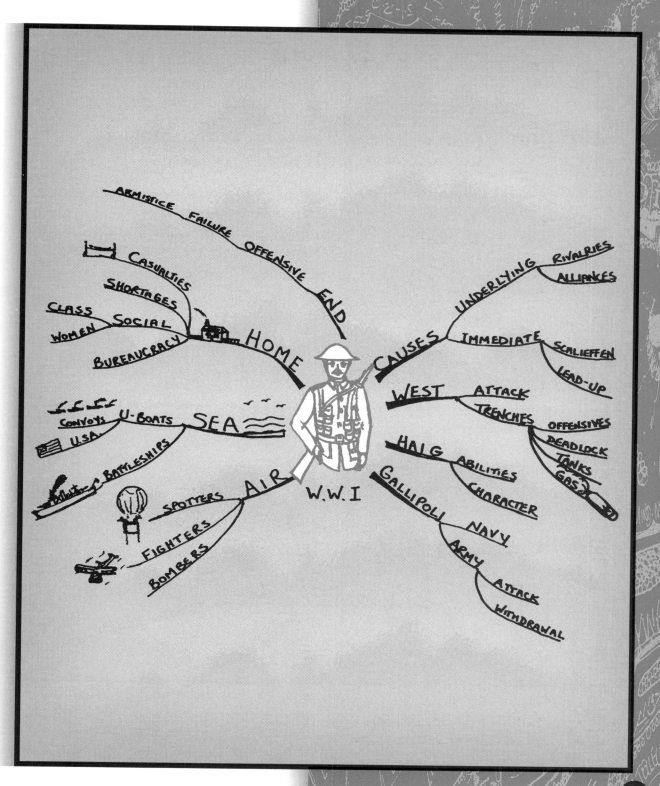

preview
What you need to know

- Why war broke out in 1914

- The war in France and Belgium

- The character and ability of Douglas Haig

- Why Allied troops landed at Gallipoli and what happened as a result

- The part played by air forces in the war

- The naval war

- How the war affected life in Britain

- How the war ended

The causes of the war

Underlying causes

Between 1870 and 1914 the new German Empire upset Britain, France and Russia. The Mind Map will remind you of the issues.

At the same time, Austria Hungary was on bad terms with Russia over the Balkans, a collection of newly independent countries. Both Austria and Russia wanted to dominate them.

Russia, Germany, Austria, France and Britain all feared that their enemies might attack them. So they made treaties to protect themselves.

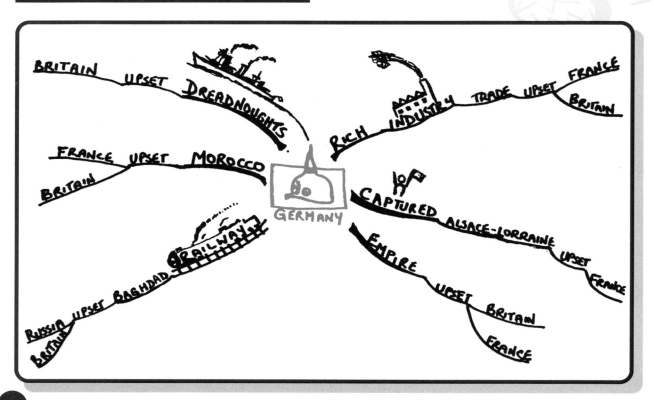

Treaty timetable

1879 Germany allied with Austria. (In 1913 the German Kaiser told the Austrian government: '*You can be certain I stand behind you, and am ready to draw the sword whenever your action makes it necessary*'.)

1891 Russia allied with France. (In 1892 the Czar of Russia wrote: '*In case of war between France and Germany we must hurl ourselves upon the Germans*'.)

1904 Britain allied with France. (In 1906 the British Foreign Minister wrote: '*The British people would not tolerate France's being involved in a war with Germany.... Any English government would be forced to help France*'.)

Specimen question

If war broke out in Europe after 1904, which countries would have been bound to fight **(a)** on Germany's side **(b)** against Germany? Explain your answer.　　　　　　　　[4 marks]

Europe in 1914

The outbreak of war

The Schlieffen Plan

When France and Russia made their treaty it meant that, if there was a war, Germany would have to fight on two fronts. In 1905 Field Marshall Alfred Von Schlieffen worked out a plan to cope with this. The timetable below and map will remind you of its main features.

The Schlieffen Plan was very risky. It depended on Russia taking a long time to mobilise. It also ignored the fact that Britain had promised (1839) to defend Belgium if she was attacked.

The lead-up to war

None of the governments wanted a large-scale war in 1914. A series of events pushed them into it. The timetable is on the right.

Schlieffen timetable

(Note: This is the order in which events were meant to happen.)

1 War breaks out.

2 Russia begins to mobilise.

3 Germany masses troops on the Belgian border.

4 France attacks Germany through Alsace-Lorraine.

5 Germany smashes south through Belgium and cuts off Paris.

6 France surrenders.

7 German troops travel by rail to fight the Russians in the east.

The outbreak of war timetable

28 June	Gavrilo Princip, a Serb, assassinated Archduke Franz Ferdinand. Austria blamed Serbia.
23 July	Austria sent Serbia ten demands. Russia advised Serbia to give way.
25 July	Serbia accepted eight out of ten.
26 July	<u>Austria declared war on Serbia</u>.
30 July	Russia began to mobilise.
31 July	Germany told Russia to stop.
1 August	Russia refused. <u>Germany declared war on Russia</u>.
2 August	<u>Germany declared war on France</u> and asked Belgium for permission to march through.
3 August	Belgium refused and asked for Britain's help.
4 August	Germany marched into Belgium and refused to withdraw. <u>Britain declared war on Germany</u>.

Notes

Remember why these events followed each other:

- Princip assassinated Franz Ferdinand because he wanted Austria to move out of Bosnia and Herzegovina.

- The Austrians attacked Serbia because they wanted to extend Austria's influence in the Balkans.

- Russia mobilised because she wanted to prevent Austria taking over in the Balkans.

- Germany declared war on Russia and France because the Schlieffen Plan depended on Germany defeating France before Russia had time to mobilise.

- Britain declared war because Germany invaded Belgium, which Britain had promised to protect.

The most likely questions about the outbreak of the First World War will concentrate either on why the European powers were on such bad terms after 1900, or on the events leading to war in 1914. To answer the questions below you need to consider the author of each source, the circumstances under which it was written/spoken and your own knowledge of the situation.

Source A

Just for a word Britain is going to make war on a kindred nation that asks only friendship. Just for a word: "neutrality"! Just for a scrap of paper!'

German Chancellor speaking to the British Ambassador, 4 August 1914

Source B

'I never doubted that, if the Germans interfered with the ... independence of Belgium, we were in honour bound to discharge our treaty obligations to that country.'

David Lloyd George (British Cabinet Minister in 1914): *War Memoirs* (1933)

Source C

'Which of us cares about Serbia? Which of us wants to see Europe at war because of these savages in the Balkans? There is probably not a single Englishman who wants war under these circumstances.'

Letter in the *Daily Mirror*, 3 August 1914

Source D

'If the German navy ever became superior to ours, the German army can conquer this country.'

Sir Edward Grey, British Foreign Minister: Memo to George V (1912)

Specimen question

Study Sources A and B. Are the two sources convincing evidence of what the German and British governments thought about Belgian neutrality in 1914? Explain your answer. [9 marks]

Model answer

Source A shows that the German government did not think that the promises made in 1839 to protect Belgium mattered. It was spoken by the head of the German government when face to face with the British ambassador. He seems to have been upset, and what he said seems to show that his government did not take international treaties seriously. He had no motive for saying this if it was not true. So it probably was. Lloyd George's statement shows that he and the government took the promises made to Belgium seriously. He wrote it many years later, in a book which he hoped would make people think well of him. So it may not be true. But it fits in with what is known about the British government's attitude from other sources. So it is probably reliable.

Specimen question

Does Source C prove that Britain would not have entered the First World War if Germany had withdrawn from Belgium on 4 August 1914? Explain your answer.   [6 marks]

Model answer

Source C is from a letter to a newspaper. It proves only what the writer of the letter thought. But it does show that some people in Britain were very unwilling to go to war over Austria's treatment of Serbia. But even if Germany had not invaded Belgium, or had withdrawn when threatened by Britain, the British government would still probably have had to go to war because of the Anglo-French treaty of 1904. The source shows that this might have been unpopular with some people. Germany's invasion of Belgium made the declaration of war more popular in Britain than it would have been otherwise.

Specimen question

Use your own knowledge of the period and the sources to explain why Britain and Germany were on such bad terms in 1914.   [15 marks]

Hints

To get high marks on this question you need to blend together information from the sources with what you already know. Writing out your notes on the topic will not be enough. Remember to concentrate on Germany's relations with <u>Britain</u>. You will get no marks for saying how she annoyed France or Russia. The Mind Map shows how you might plan your answer.

check

that you understand how and why war broke out in August 1914.

The Western Front

The German attack

When the war began, the Germans put the Schlieffen Plan into effect, but it did not work (*see* map). This was partly because the German High Command did not use as many troops to attack France as Von Schlieffen had planned.

Notes

The map below contains a lot of information. It shows how:

1 The Germans drove south from Belgium.

2 The French:
   (i) moved their army from the Alsace-Lorraine front to block the Germans on the River Marne,
   (ii) brought out an army from Paris.

3 The British forces first fought against the Germans at Mons, and then retreated to link up with the French on the Marne.

4 The Allies stopped the German advance at the Battle of the Marne (September 1914).

check

Maps can help you to understand and remember. Try drawing your own to help with your revision.

Source

'Our men are done in. For four days they have been marching 40 km a day ... They march with their eyes closed, singing in chorus so that they shall not fall asleep on the march.'

A German officer quoted in John Terraine: *Mons* (1960)

Specimen question

What evidence is there that the speed of the French retreat made things difficult for the Germans?

[3 marks]

Trench warfare

After the Battle of the Marne the two opposing armies established lines of trenches stretching from the English Channel to the Swiss frontier. The Mind Map will remind you of the main features of trench warfare.

The key features of trench warfare were lines of trenches strongly defended by barbed wire and machine guns. Generals on both sides wanted to break through. Attacks on trenches cost enormous numbers of lives. On the first day of the Battle of the Somme in 1916, 20,000 British troops were killed and 40,000 injured. One battalion lost 497 men out of 730 in one day. Ludendorff described the situation in the trenches in 1917: *'It was no longer life, it was mere unspeakable suffering.'*

Source A

'A series of extended lines of infantry were seen moving forward from the British trenches … They came at a steady, easy pace, as if expecting to find nothing alive in our front trenches … When the British line was within a hundred metres the rattle of machine gun and rifle broke out along the whole line … Immediately afterwards a mass of shells from the German batteries in rear tore through the air and burst among the advancing lines … All along the line men could be seen throwing up their arms and collapsing, never to move again … Again and again the extended lines of British infantry broke against the German defence like waves against a cliff, only to be beaten back.'

M Gerster: *Die Swaben an der Ancre* (1920)

Source B

'I awoke with a tremendous start, conscious of noise, incessant and almost musical, so intense that it seemed as if a hundred devils were dancing in my brain. Everything seemed to be vibrating – the ground, my dug-out, my bed.'

Arthur Behrend, describing being bombarded

Source C

'The ground between our trench and the ruins beyond was merely a stretch of craters and burnt-out grass broken up by tangled wire, not unlike gorse bushes. The dead were lying there in all conceivable attitudes, rotting in the sun.'

Paul Maze, A French soldier, writing in 1932

Source D

'If you want the old battalion,
We know where they are
They're hanging on the old barbed wire.'

A First World War British army marching song

Specimen questions

1 Read Source A. What weapons destroyed the infantry's efforts to capture the enemy trenches? [3 marks]

2 How does Source B help to justify Ludendorff's description of trench warfare as 'unspeakable suffering'? [3 marks]

3 Read Source C. How did the conditions Paul Maze described hinder those attacking the trenches? [4 marks]

4 How far do the figures quoted in the introduction to the sources help to explain the words of the marching song (Source D)? Would the British military authorities have approved of the song? Explain your answer. [6 marks]

New weapons

Two new weapons were tried to break the deadlock:

★ **Poison gas**
This failed because sometimes the wind changed and blew the gas back on the attackers, and gas masks were developed to neutralise it.

★ **Tanks**
These were used to drive straight over the trenches. Tanks failed because they were slow and unreliable and got stuck in the mud. And even if they broke through, the following infantry still had to face machine guns.

In spite of the lack of success, the attacks continued.

Western Front offensives timetable

Date	Place	Casualties	Comments
1916 (Feb–Jun)	Verdun (German)	F 315,000 G 280,000	Aimed to destroy Verdun and break French army. Failed
1916 (Jul–Nov)	Somme (Allied)	A 790,000 G 540,000	Dented the German lines slightly.
1917 (April)	Aisne (French)	A 270,000	French driven back; 750,000 of them mutinied.
1917 (Jul–Nov)	Passchendaele (British)	B 500,000 G 270,000	Dented the German line.

NB The aim of all the offensives, except Verdun, was to break through. Casualty figures (F = French, G = German, A = Allied, B = British) are approximate. Also remember that many soldiers were injured on several occasions and were counted as casualties every time.

Notes

Notice how much information can be crammed into a table. Compile your own tables to help with your revision. Use the table and the sources to find out:

1 What happened at Verdun in 1916?

2 When and where did French troops mutiny?

3 What reasons did they have for mutinying?

4 Were the attacks on the Somme and Passchendaele successes or failures? Give reasons for your answers.

Source A

'The story is the same story I have had to tell so many times, the story of an attack pushed with perfect determination and gallantry to final and complete success.'

Report in *The Times*, October 1917

Source B

'Still the guns churned this treacherous slime. Every day conditions grew worse. What had once been difficult now became impossible.'

General Hubert Gough, writing of the October 1917 attack: *The Fifth Army* (1931)

Source C

Lines of grey, muttering faces, marked with fear,
They leave the trenches, going over the top,
While time ticks blank and busy on their wrists,
And hope, with furtive eyes and grappling fists,
Flounders in mud. O Jesus, make it stop!

Siegfried Sassoon: *Counter-Attack* (1918)

Source D

No Man's Land in Passchendaele in 1917

Specimen question

Sources A and B both describe the Battle of Passchendaele in 1917. To what extent do they contradict each other? Which do you consider is the more reliable? Explain your answer using the other sources and your own knowledge. [9 marks]

Hints

To show how they contradict each other, compare 'final and complete success' in Source A with 'impossible' in Source B. Source A was written by a journalist. Where did he get his information? Was this likely to be a reliable source? Who were his readers? What did they want to read? Why? Source B was written by a British general many years later. Was he likely to minimise the success of British troops? Which of the two does Source D seem to support? In any case, from your own knowledge, what was the result of the battle of Passchendaele?

Specimen question

Source C is from a poem written by an officer who served in the trenches. What can it tell us about fighting on the Western Front? [6 marks]

Model answer

Source C is a poem about feelings. It tells us what Sassoon thought people felt when they were going over the top in an attack. It gives the impression that they felt ill, that they were frightened, that time meant nothing to them, and that as they floundered in the mud they lost all hope and prayed for it all to stop. Sassoon had lived in the trenches, and knew what it was like. In any case, the feelings he describes seem reasonable under

the circumstances, and fit in with other accounts, so it is probably an accurate account of what many infantrymen felt like when attacking.

Specimen question

Using the sources and your own knowledge, explain why trench warfare resulted in years of deadlock. [12 marks]

Hints

Use all the information mentioned in the section on trench warfare to show how strong trench defences were compared with the forces available to attack them. Use Sources B and D to highlight the effects of bombardments and the limited usefulness of tanks. Source C will show how pointless many of the infantry thought it was to attack. Any system where defence is so much stronger than attack is bound to lead to deadlock. You would get extra credit for pointing out that trench warfare in the American Civil War (1861–5) led to much the same problem. Examiners like you to be able to show how the events you are describing fit in with other times and other places.

check

that you understand how trench warfare resulted in deadlock.

Douglas Haig

Douglas Haig was the British Commander in Chief. He and his staff played a very important part in deciding how the war should be fought.

Source A

'We have inflicted very heavy losses on the enemy … In another 6 weeks the enemy should be hard put to it to find men … The maintenance of a steady offensive pressure will result eventually in his complete overthrow.'

Douglas Haig: *Diary* (August 1916)

Source B

'I told [a general] that I thought the German was now nearly at his last resources and that there was only <u>one sound</u> plan to follow, viz., <u>without delay</u> to

1 Send to France every possible man

2 Send to France every possible aeroplane

3 Send to France every possible gun.'

Douglas Haig: *Diary* (June 1917)

Source C

'Blood and mud, blood and mud, they can think of nothing better.'

Lloyd George, British Prime Minister, speaking of British generals in September 1917.

Source D

'Unfortunately Haig placed complete confidence in General Charteris, head of his Intelligence Service … Charteris always told Haig something he especially wanted to hear: … that there were no Germans on our front, or that they were … exhausted. These misconceptions … cost the British army dearly.'

General Hubert Gough: *Soldiering On* (1954)

Specimen question

Haig was accused of being too optimistic, obstinate and unimaginative. How far do Sources A, B and C support this accusation?   [6 marks]

Hint

Remember when the war, in fact, ended. Was Haig's view in 1916 and 1917 optimistic? Remember the Battle of the Somme in 1916. Was it obstinate of Haig to want more resources in France in 1917? Lloyd George clearly thought Haig and the other generals were unimaginative. But what alternatives to 'blood and mud' were there?

Specimen question

How far does Source D

(a) explain

(b) excuse Haig's optimism?

[4 marks]

check

What do you think of Douglas Haig? Can you defend your view?

Gallipoli

At the end of 1914 the Russians asked Britain to help in the war against Turkey. The government decided to attack the Dardanelles. Winston Churchill, who helped to organise the attack, thought it would be better *'than sending our armies to chew barbed wire in Flanders'*.

In all, the Gallipoli campaign cost the Allies more than 200,000 dead, sick and wounded, and a huge amount of ammunition and supplies. It gained nothing.

Specimen question

The Gallipoli campaign made it easier for Haig to argue that all available forces should be sent to France. Why was this?   [4 marks]

check

that you understand what happened at Gallipoli, and what the results were.

Gallipoli timetable

March 1915	Naval attack on Dardanelles.
	Then Turks strengthened defences.
April 1915	Allied troops landed on five Cape Helles beaches and Anzac Cove.
	Failed to advance inland.
August 1915	Allied troops landed at Suvla Bay.
	Failed to advance inland.
December 1915	Troops withdrawn from Anzac and Suvla.
January 1916	Troops withdrawn from Helles.

The Gallipoli campaign

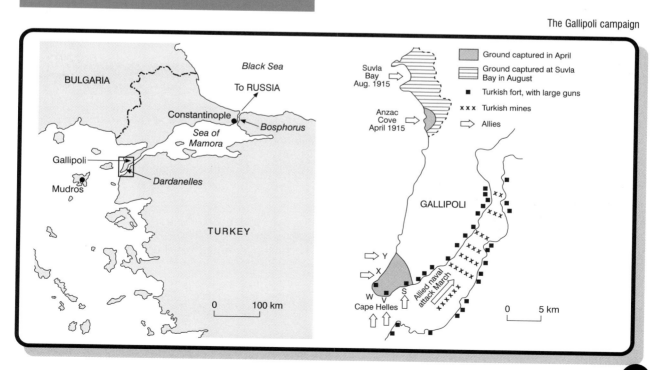

The air war

The Mind Map will remind you of the main features of the air war.

Notes

At the beginning of the war, aeroplanes were light and flimsy and were used, together with balloons, for observing the enemy lines from the air. Faster and stronger machines were developed. Some were fighters, which fought air battles. Skilled pilots were known as 'aces'.

At the beginning of the war, Germany possessed a number of airships called Zeppelins which bombed British towns, causing damage and casualties. Later in the war aeroplanes were powerful enough to carry bombs, and both Britain and Germany used them to raid enemy territory.

But war in the air played only a small part in the First World War.

check

that you understand developments in the air war.

The war at sea

The Mind Map on the next page will remind you of the main points of the war at sea.

Notes

Before the war Germany and Britain both spent huge sums of money on Dreadnought battleships which were expected to play an important part in the war. But, partly because they were so expensive, Dreadnoughts spent most of the war in harbour. The most important part was played by submarines.

Specimen questions

Use the timetable to answer the following questions:

1. Both Germany and Britain claimed to have won the Battle of Jutland. How could that be?
   [6 marks]

2. The German navy took a great risk in 1917, which did not come off. Explain. [6 marks]

check

that you understand the part played by the navies in the war.

Navy timetable

1914	British	Blockaded Germany throughout the war.
	British	Falklands: Sank German ships trying to return from the Pacific.
1915	German	Ultimatum that U-boats would, without warning, sink ships approaching Britain. Sank *Lusitania*, killing 128 Americans. Germans withdrew warning.
1916	German	Fleet put to sea. So did British. Battle of Jutland. British lost more ships, but Germans went back to port and stayed there.
1917	German	New U-boat warning. Sank ships (including US) on way to Britain. At first very successful.
	British	Organised ships into convoys. Cut losses.
	USA	Declared war on Germany.

The Home Front

Before the war broke out in 1914, Sir Edward Grey said *'If we are engaged in a war we shall suffer but little more that we shall suffer if we stand aside.'* In fact the war hit Britain hard, and brought about many changes (see Mind Map).

Notes

★ **Bureaucracy**
A J P Taylor, the historian, wrote that *'until 1914 a sensible, law abiding Englishman could pass through life and hardly notice the existence of the state, beyond the post office and the policeman.'* By the end of the war the state was interfering in everyday lives in all the areas mentioned in the Mind Map.

★ **Morals**
The horrors of war made many people lose their faith in God. The uncertainty of life, particularly for soldiers, led some young people to enjoy sex as often as possible while they could.

★ **Class**
Social classes mingled more in the war than ever before, in hospitals, factories and in the trenches. This helped to break down rigid class barriers.

★ **Women**
Four million young men joined the forces during the war and had to be replaced in the workforce. The number of women working in trade and industry increased by over a million. Their work was essential, and helped to win them respect and the vote. In addition their pay made them more independent.

★ **Casualties**
Combined casualties from bombardments and air raids were 1,550 killed and 4,733 wounded.

★ **Shortages**
The U-boat war, especially in 1917, led to shortages of some sorts of food, which were rationed in 1918. There were also shortages of coal and coke.

Source A

British Women! — the Royal Air Force needs your help

as CLERKS, WAITRESSES, COOKS, experienced MOTOR CYCLISTS & in many other capacities. Full particulars from the nearest EMPLOYMENT EXCHANGE ENROL AT ONCE IN THE W·R·A·F. WOMEN'S ROYAL AIR FORCE

1918 WRAF recruiting poster

Source B

'In this war [women] have invaded the spheres hitherto considered sacred to men … and they have done all these things with an efficiency which has surprised and delighted the whole nation.'

Neville Chamberlain (Director of National Service): Speech, 1917

Source C

'By the end of the war, it was no longer true that woman's place was in the home.'

A J P Taylor: *The First World War* (1963)

Specimen question

Study Sources A and B. To what extent do they show that women's work and people's opinions about them changed in the war? Explain your answer.   [9 marks]

Model answer

Before the war, the idea of a woman joining a branch of the fighting services would have seemed very strange. On the other hand, the poster (Source A) emphasises posts as clerks, waitresses and cooks, all jobs that women might have done before the war. But they would not have been employed as motor cyclists. Neville Chamberlain's speech shows that by 1917 women had taken over men's jobs in civilian life and done them well. But he was 'surprised and delighted' that they had been able to do this. So before the war he must have had a low opinion of their abilities. So the two sources show that during the war women joined the forces, did work hitherto only done by men and that as a result people had a higher opinion of them than before.

Specimen question

Using the sources and your own knowledge, explain briefly what women did during the war to justify A J P Taylor's claim. To what extent was the claim still true after the war?   [12 marks]

Hints

Notice that you are asked to 'explain' what women did during the war, not to list their contributions. So you need to think carefully how to present all the information briefly. How about the following points?

1 Was it ever true that 'woman's place was in the home'? What about textile workers and elementary teachers?

2 But many more women took work outside the home during the war.

3 Some did jobs created by the war – for example in the forces (Source A) and munitions factories.

4 Some replaced the men who had gone into the forces. This involved lots of different jobs. You would not be expected to give more than a few examples.

5 At the end of the war the men wanted their jobs back and the wartime jobs disappeared.

6 As a result many women lost their jobs and went back to their 'places' in the home. But they got the vote, which showed that it was taken for granted that they had some interests outside the home.

check

that you understand how the war changed life in Britain.

The end of the war

Two events in 1917 broke the deadlock and ended the war. The USA declared war on Germany, and the new revolutionary government in Russia made peace with Germany.

Ludendorff decided to use the German troops who had been fighting in Russia to attack and defeat the French and British armies in France before the Americans could come and help them.

Ludendorff attacked in March 1918. The map will remind you of what happened. Notice how, for the first time since 1914, the Germans broke through. Then in August, the Allies counter-attacked and drove them back.

At the same time there were strikes in German towns and the navy mutinied. In November the German government surrendered.

Source A

'Our troops are exhausted and their numbers have dwindled terribly ... They surrender in hordes whenever the enemy attacks. Whatever happens we must obtain peace, before the enemy breaks through into Germany.'

Crown Prince Rupprecht of Bavaria, a German General: Report (18 October 1918)

Source B

'The war was now lost ... After the way in which our troops on the western front had been used up, we had to count on being driven back again and again. Our situation could only get worse, never better.'

General Ludendorff's evidence to a postwar Reichstag committee

The front line in 1918

HOLLAND

UK + Belgium (Sept.)

Lys

Scheldt

Ypres

BELGIUM

Meuse

GERMANY

FRANCE

March 1918

UK (Sept.)

Somme

March 1918

Amiens

LUXEMBOURG

May 1918

UK (Aug.)

French (Aug.)

French (Aug.)

Reims

Verdun

Oise

French

Seine

Marne

USA (Sept.)

Paris

USA (Aug.)

French (Aug.)

French + USA

Legend	
✕—✕—✕ Front line in March 1918	⬅ Germans
•••• Front line in November 1918	⬜ Allies
▦ Area captured by Germans	

0   60 km

Specimen question

check

that you understand why the war ended in 1918.

After the war, many Germans, including Hitler, said that the German army had not been defeated, but had been 'stabbed in the back' by the politicians who had surrendered unnecessarily. Does Prince Rupprecht's report prove Hitler wrong? Explain your answer.   [6 marks]

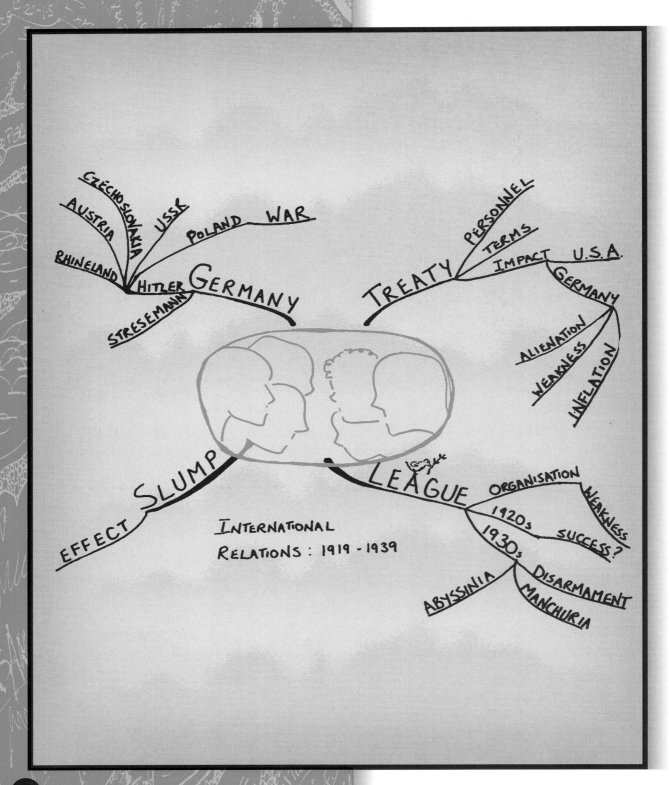

CZECHOSLOVAKIA
AUSTRIA
USSR
POLAND   WAR
RHINELAND
HITLER GERMANY
STRESEMANN

TREATY PERSONNEL
TERMS
IMPACT   U.S.A.
GERMANY
ALIENATION
WEAKNESS
INFLATION

EFFECT SLUMP

INTERNATIONAL
RELATIONS: 1919 - 1939

LEAGUE   ORGANISATION   WEAKNESS
1920s   SUCCESS?
1930s   DISARMAMENT
ABYSSINIA   MANCHURIA

preview
What you need to know

- How the peace treaties were made and what the terms were

- How the peace treaty affected Germany

- Why the League of Nations was founded, how it was organised and how successful it was

- How the Depression affected peace keeping

- German foreign policy before and after Hitler came to power in 1933

The peace treaties

The peace treaties after the First World War were made by three leaders. You need to know who they were, what they wanted and how strong they were.

★ USA President Wilson
He wanted above all to make sure that there would never be another war. He thought every nation had the right to be free and self-governing, and that a League of Nations should be set up to settle disputes between countries. He represented the strongest and richest country in the world. This gave him great power.

★ British Prime Minister Lloyd George
He wanted a just peace. He said, *'We must not allow any sense of revenge, any grasping desire to override the spirit of righteousness.'* But his power depended on British MPs. Most of them wanted Germany to be punished.

★ French Prime Minister Clemençeau
Clemençeau, supported by the majority of the French, wanted to regain Alsace-Lorraine and to weaken Germany so that it would never again be able to attack France.

Five treaties were signed at the end of the war (*see* Mind Map). Germany was not allowed to take part in the negotiations.

Europe before the 1919 treaties

- NORWAY
- SWEDEN
- GREAT BRITAIN
- DENMARK
- HOLLAND
- RUSSIAN EMPIRE
- GERMAN EMPIRE
- BELGIUM
- LUXEMBOURG
- FRANCE
- AUSTRO-HUNGARIAN EMPIRE
- SWITZERLAND
- PORTUGAL
- SPAIN
- ITALY
- ROMANIA
- MONTENEGRO
- SERBIA
- BULGARIA
- ALBANIA
- GREECE
- TURKISH EMPIRE

Europe after the 1919 treaties

- NORWAY
- SWEDEN
- FINLAND
- GREAT BRITAIN
- ESTONIA
- LATVIA
- LITHUANIA
- DENMARK
- HOLLAND
- GERMANY (EAST PRUSSIA)
- RUSSIA
- BELGIUM
- GERMANY
- POLAND
- LUXEMBOURG
- CZECHOSLOVAKIA
- FRANCE
- AUSTRIA
- HUNGARY
- SWITZERLAND
- ROMANIA
- PORTUGAL
- SPAIN
- ITALY
- YUGOSLAVIA
- BULGARIA
- ALBANIA
- GREECE
- TURKEY
- SYRIA
- LEBANON

Notes

The maps show the territorial changes made in the treaties. Notice how much information a map can contain. Try drawing your own and colour code the individual countries to help with your revision.

Compare the two maps. Notice:

1
- The land which Germany lost, and who got it.
- What happened to Austria/Hungary.
- The land lost by the USSR and who got it.
- The land lost by Bulgaria, and who got it.
- The land lost by Turkey in the Middle East.

2 Czechoslovakia, Poland and Austria all contained people who thought of themselves as German.

3 Yugoslavia and Czechoslovakia were both 'new' countries containing a mixture of nationalities. What has happened to them in recent years?

Problems with the treaty

Germany also had to agree to other terms (*see* Mind Map). At first the German government refused to accept the terms of the treaty, but was told that it had to. The US Congress thought the treaty was too severe, and refused to ratify it.

Source A

'You may strip Germany of her colonies, reduce her army to a mere police force and her navy to that of a fifth-rate power. All the same ... if she feels she has been unjustly treated ... she will find means of exacting retribution from her conqueror.'

Ex Prime Minister Lloyd George: Speech (1923)

Source B

'The treaty was not so grand, I am quite willing to admit that, but how about the war? Was it so *very* grand? ... France came out of it alive, her territory recovered, her colonial empire increased, while Germany was broken and disarmed.'

Ex French Prime Minister Clemençeau in an interview in 1928

Source C

PEACE AND FUTURE CANNON FODDER

The Tiger : " *Curious! I seem to hear a child weeping!* "

A cartoon published in the *Daily Herald*. ('The Class of 1940' refers to those who would be old enough to join the army to fight in 1940.)

Specimen questions

1 What fears did Lloyd George and the *Daily Herald* cartoonist have about the peace treaties? Explain your answer. [6 marks]

2 Is it fair to say that Lloyd George looked forward, while Clemençeau seemed not to care about the future? Explain your answer. [4 marks]

check

that you understand the terms of the Treaty of Versailles.

Germany 1919–23

Popularity of the government

The fact that the new democratic German government had signed the Treaty of Versailles made them unpopular.

Specimen question

In what ways did the Treaty of Versailles limit Germany's military strength? [4 marks]

Hints

To earn four marks you need to mention four restrictions (e.g. no air force, no large battleships, no heavy artillery, no U-boats). Always notice the number of marks on offer. For four marks you will not be expected to write a long, full answer.

Specimen question

Why did the victors want to weaken Germany? [6 marks]

Hint

To earn six marks you need to give several reasons, explain them and link them together.

Model answer

The victors wanted to weaken Germany because they feared that there might be another war, and thought that weakening Germany was the best way of preventing one. They also wanted to punish Germany, whom they blamed for starting the war. Weakening Germany was a good way to punish her.

So, for example, cutting Germany's armed forces and occupying the Rhineland seemed good ways to punish Germany and to protect France.

Specimen question

'Reparations were the most important reason why Germany hated the Treaty of Versailles.' Do you agree with this statement? Explain your answer. [10 marks]

Hint

If you deal only with the reason mentioned in a question like this, you will score less than half marks. To score full marks you need to explain that all or most of the terms were unpopular in Germany, and that it is just not enough to pick out one 'most important' reason.

Model answer

Germans hated the Treaty of Versailles because it was a humiliation for their country and made some of them suffer. It was humiliating to lose their colonies and to have their army and navy reduced in size. It was humiliating to have to hand Alsace-Lorraine back to France, to lose Danzig and to have foreign troops occupying the Rhineland and the French running the Saar coal fields. It was also very humiliating to have to accept the blame for starting the war, and to have to pay reparations to the Allies when Germany needed money to rebuild its industries and provide jobs after the war. So all the terms of the treaty, coupled with the fact that it was imposed on them without asking what they thought, combined to make Germans hate it. It is wrong to single out one clause.

Make a Mind Map of the main points contained in this answer.

Economy

The German government also failed to control the country's economy.

Inflation timetable

1919	1 dollar = 14 marks.	
1921	Reparations fixed at £6,600 million.	
1922	German payments fell behind.	
1923	**January**	French and Belgian troops occupied the Ruhr to enforce payment.
		1 dollar = 18,000 marks.
	September	1 dollar = 98 million marks.
	November	1 dollar = 4,200 billion marks.

Notes

When Germany's reparation payments fell behind and French and Belgian troops took over German factories and mines in the Ruhr, people thought that marks were certain to drop in value and sold them. This reduced their value.

To make up for this the German government printed more marks. This reduced their value still further, so even more were printed. And so the process went on, faster and faster.

Source A

'In the summer of that inflation year my grandmother … [sold] her house for I don't know how many thousands of millions of marks … Nothing was left except a pile of worthless pieces of paper when she died a few months later.'

Egon Larsen: *Weimar Eyewitness* (1976)

Source B

'All [ordinary people] knew was that a large bank account could not buy a straggly bunch of carrots … They knew that as individuals they were bankrupt. And they knew hunger when it gnawed at them, as it did daily. In their misery and their hopelessness they made the Republic the scapegoat for all that had happened.'

William L Shirer: *The Rise and Fall of the Third Reich* (1959)

Specimen question

Why, according to the sources, was the German government unpopular at the end of 1923? How far could this be blamed on the terms of the Versailles Treaty? [6 marks]

Hint

As a rule in questions based on sources, you can use your general knowledge of the period in your answer. In this case you must use only information contained in the sources when answering the first part of the question.

check

that you understand the effect the Versailles Treaty had on Germany.

The League of Nations

Establishment

The First World War was a catastrophe. It killed 10 million people and wounded 20 million. It was also very expensive. It cost Britain about £7,000 million. To try to prevent war, the Treaty of Versailles set up the League of Nations to settle disputes between countries by negotiation. The USA refused to join, and Germany, Russia and Turkey were excluded. The League could only use blockades to enforce its decisions. It had no armed forces at its disposal.

Organisation

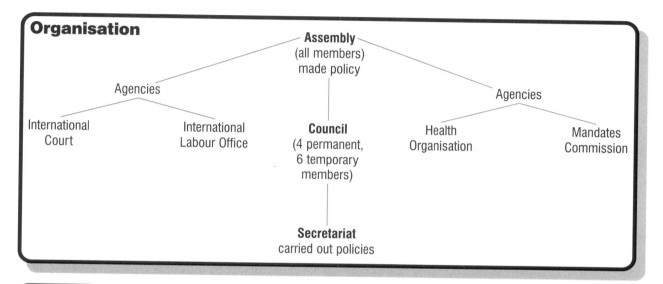

Assembly
(all members)
made policy

Agencies

International Court

International Labour Office

Council
(4 permanent, 6 temporary members)

Agencies

Health Organisation

Mandates Commission

Secretariat
carried out policies

Source

THE GAP IN THE BRIDGE.

A cartoon published in *Punch* (10 December 1919)

2

Specimen question

What does the cartoonist in the source think about the League of Nations? Back up your answer by referring to details in the cartoon.

[5 marks]

Hints

What points is the cartoonist trying to make, and how does he use details in the cartoon to make them? For example, the League was greatly weakened by the absence of the USA – the missing keystone being the most important piece of the bridge. And though a US president, Woodrow Wilson, founded the League, as shown on the sign, the US government, lounging on the bank, were threatening the whole structure by refusing to join.

Specimen question

What did the Great Powers want the League of Nations to achieve? [5 marks]

Hint

If you know a lot about the foundation of the League you could easily write too much on this. Remember, no matter how much you write, you won't get more than five marks. All that is needed for five marks is something like the following model answer.

Model answer

The Great Powers wanted the League to prevent wars by making sure that all disputes were settled by negotiation, and by making it easier for member states to band together to help other members if they were attacked. They also wanted the League to deal with other problems which arose from the peace treaties, such as controlling the administration of the mandated territories and dealing with refugees.

Source

Lord Robert Cecil, one of the founders of the League of Nations, wrote:

'The governments had agreed to the covenant [of the League] without taking it seriously. To them any genuine attempt to apply its provisions … was "midsummer madness".'

Viscount Cecil: Letter to Winston Churchill (1944)

Specimen question

If Lord Cecil was right, could the League have ever succeeded? Explain your answer. [4 marks]

check

that you understand the weaknesses of the League.

The League in the 1920s

Between 1919 and 1930 the League was involved in various disputes (*see* timetable).

Notes

- Germany was annoyed in 1921 because the League handed over some German Silesians to be ruled by Poland.

- The League's decision over Corfu was unpopular because many people believed that Italy won only because it was a permanent member of the Council and Greece was not.

- Under the Dawes Plan, the USA lent Germany money to pay reparations.

- The League ordered Poland and Lithuania to negotiate over the future of Vilna, captured by Poland. Poland refused and kept Vilna.

- The League tried to supervise the way in which the Allies administered 'mandated' territories. But they took no notice.

Notice how much information a table can contain. Try compiling your own to help with your revision. You would not be expected to know details of all the disputes mentioned in the table. Half a dozen or so will do.

Specimen question

How successful was the League of Nations in settling disputes between 1920 and 1930? Explain your answer. [6 marks]

League 1920s timetable

Date	Place/Problem	Issue	Rivals	Result	Comment
1919	Alands	ownership	Sweden *v* Finland	Finland won	success
1920	Schleswig	ownership	Denmark *v* Germany	plebiscite split	success
1921	Silesia	ownership	Poland *v* Germany	plebiscite split	annoyed Germany
1922	S America	borders	Columbia *v* Venezuela	decided	success
1923	Corfu	compensation	Italy *v* Greece	Italy won	unpopular
1924	reparations	payment	Germany *v* Allies	Dawes Plan	success
1925	Balkans	Greek invasion	Greece *v* Bulgaria	Greeks withdrew	success
1925	S America	borders	Chile *v* Peru	decided	success
1926	Mosul	ownership	Iraq *v* Turkey	Iraq won	success
1927	Vilna	ownership	Poland *v* Lithuania	Poland won	League ignored
1920–30	mandates	supervision	League *v* Allies	no effect	League ignored

Hints

Approach this kind of question by making a statement and then giving an example. For instance, you could say that the League was very successful in settling minor disputes between small countries, giving a couple of examples, but was helpless when one of the parties refused to do what it was told (e.g. Poland) or when it had to deal with stronger countries (e.g. Italy). In these cases it was shown to be weak and ineffective. So it was only partly successful.

The League of Nations 1930–9

After 1930 the League faced very difficult problems, which it could not solve (*see* Mind Map).

★ Disarmament
Disarmament seemed a good way to prevent wars, so in 1929 the British Labour government persuaded the League to organise a disarmament conference which met from 1932 to 1934. It failed. (*see* diagram).

★ Manchuria
In 1931 Japan invaded Manchuria. China asked the League for help. The League set up a commission under Lord Lytton. This said that Japan should withdraw. Japan refused and left the League.

★ Abyssinia
In 1935 Mussolini, the Italian dictator, invaded Abyssinia, whose ruler, Haile Selassie, asked the League for help. In response, 52 nations agreed not to lend money or sell weapons to Italy. But they went on selling oil to Italy. Italy took over the whole country and resigned from the League.

Germany wanted to rearm. In 1933 Hitler came to power and withdrew from the League

Japan's invasion of Manchuria made people think disarmament was dangerous

Failure of conference

France wanted to keep strong enough forces to fight off Germany

A new British government elected in 1931 was against disarmament

THE ULTIMATUM.

JAPAN. "IF YOU GO ON SAYING I'M NAUGHTY, I SHALL LEAVE THE CLASS."

A cartoon published in *Punch* (7 December 1932)

Specimen question

Look at Source A. What impression does the artist give of the firmness shown by the League and Japan's reaction to the League? Explain your answer. [5 marks]

Hint

Organise your answer along the lines of the model answer on page 28. Identify what points the cartoonist is trying to make, then show how he uses the details in the cartoon to make them.

Specimen question

What effects did the successful invasion of Manchuria have on world opinion? [5 marks]

Hint

How effective would people think the League was? What effect would this have on leaders such as Mussolini thinking of aggression? What effect would it have on those fearing attack?

Source B

'If the League … had extended sanctions to oil, I would have had to withdraw from Abyssinia within a week.'

Mussolini looking back on the invasion of Abyssinia

Source C

'This was the death-blow to the League as well as to Abyssinia. Fifty-two nations had combined to resist aggression; all they accomplished was that Haile Selassie lost all his country … One day [the League] was a powerful body imposing sanctions … the next day it was an empty sham.'

A J P Taylor: *The Origins of the Second World War* (1961)

Specimen questions

Look at Sources B and C.

1 How might the League have made sanctions against Italy more effective? Explain your answer. [4 marks]

2 Why did A J P Taylor describe Abyssinia as 'the death-blow' to the League? [5 marks]

check

that you can explain why the League of Nations had some success in the 1920s, but failed in the 1930s.

The Depression

In October 1929 the price of shares in US companies was higher than it had ever been. But the profits earned by companies were falling. It looked as if the price of shares might soon fall as well. So some shareholders decided to sell and the price of shares began to fall. Soon everybody was selling. Share prices fell faster and faster until many were almost worthless. Companies went bankrupt and many prosperous Americans suddenly found their investments worth nothing. This 'Wall Street Crash' had effects worldwide.

Specimen question

Why did the Wall Street Crash make it harder to prevent the outbreak of war between 1930 and 1939? Explain your answer fully.   [15 marks]

Hint

'Open-ended' questions like this are difficult to answer well. To achieve a high grade you need to show that you understand all aspects of the question, and be able to back up what you say with detailed evidence. The model answer is the kind of answer that would earn an A grade. Notice that it *selects* relevant information, which it uses to answer the question, and that it backs up general statements with particular examples.

Model answer

The Wall Street Crash caused a major slump in the USA. Many companies went bankrupt and by 1932, 12 million people were unemployed. This encouraged politicians such as Mussolini, Hitler and the Japanese generals who all believed that democratic government did not work and were prepared to use force to get their way.

The slump spread all over the world. Countries stopped lending each other money, because they feared they might not be repaid. This weakened democratic governments. During the 1920s the USA had lent money to Western Europe. Suddenly the USA wanted the money back. This hit Germany hard because she had borrowed more than 20,000 million marks from the USA to pay her war reparations. Now she had no money to finance German trade and industry. By 1932, 44 per cent of German workers were unemployed. The Weimar government seemed helpless and many Germans voted instead for Hitler, who took power in 1933. In this way the Crash helped to bring to power the man who did most to bring about war in 1939.

The slump in trade caused by the Crash also hit France and Britain. By 1932 there were three million unemployed in Britain and well over a million in France. The British and French governments decided they could not afford to spend much on armaments. As a result they did not have the power or the confidence to oppose Mussolini when he invaded Abyssinia, or to stop Hitler when he occupied the Rhineland in 1936.

The Crash also affected the Pacific area, where Japan was trying to expand its influence. Before 1930 Japan did this by trading with other countries, but the slump after the Crash ruined these plans. So the Japanese government decided to use force instead, beginning with the invasion of Manchuria in 1931, believing that the USA was now too weak to stop them.

So, in various parts of the world, the Wall Street Crash helped to strengthen dictatorships and weakened democracies, making it more difficult to keep the peace.

check

that you understand why the Depression made it more difficult to keep the peace.

German foreign policy 1924–39

The problems of the peace

Source

'First … the solution of the reparations question in a way that is tolerable for Germany, and the assurance of peace which is essential for us to recover our strength. Second, the protection of Germans abroad, those 10 to 12 million … who now live under foreign rule…. The third great task is to recover Danzig, the Polish corridor and a correction of the frontier in Upper Silesia.'

Gustav Stresemann, the German Foreign Minister, writing of his aims in September 1925

The Locarno treaty

At the end of 1925 Stresemann signed a treaty at Locarno. He promised:

1 To allow France to keep Alsace-Lorraine.

2 Not to put troops into the Rhineland.

3 Not to use force to alter the frontiers of Poland and Czechoslovakia.

As a reward Germany was invited to join the League of Nations.

Specimen question

Many Germans agreed with Stresemann's aims. Do you think they would have been pleased by the treaty he signed at Locarno? Explain your answer.

[5 marks]

Hint

As a rule it is safest to give a balanced answer to this kind of question, looking for things which might have pleased the Germans – admission to the League of Nations, for example – as well as aspects which they might not have liked such as the promises about the Rhineland and the other existing frontiers. Remember to refer back to Stresemann's aims as you go along. So you might decide that most Germans would have had mixed feelings about the treaty.

Just before he died in 1929, Stresemann agreed the Young Plan, which reduced the amount of reparations Germany had to pay by 70 per cent.

check

that you understand what Stresemann wanted to achieve and how he went about it.

Hitler's foreign policy timetable

1933 Hitler left the League of Nations, refused to pay any more reparations and began to rearm.

1936 Hitler broke the 1919 treaty by sending troops into the Rhineland. Nobody tried to stop him.

1938 (March) Hitler broke the 1919 treaty by taking over Austria. Nobody tried to stop him.
(September) The Munich agreement, negotiated by Hitler and Chamberlain, allowed Germany to take over part of Czechoslovakia.

1939 (March) Hitler took over the rest of Czechoslovakia. Nobody tried to stop him.
(August) Hitler signed a pact with the Soviet Union.
(September) Hitler invaded Poland. This started the Second World War.

Hitler's policies

In 1933 Hitler came to power in Germany. By this time the League of Nations had lost much of its prestige (*see* Manchuria page 30) He faced the same problems as Stresemann, but he took a very different line.

When you are instructed to refer to a particular source to answer a question, you can also use your own knowledge and any of the other sources if they are relevant.

Source A

'I had no army worth mentioning … If the French had taken any action we would easily have been defeated.'

Hitler, speaking afterwards about the German occupation of the Rhineland

Source B

'The Germans, after all, are only going into their own back garden.'

Lord Lothian, a British politician, speaking of the Rhineland occupation

Specimen questions

1. What, according to Hitler, would have happened if the French had opposed the German troops entering the Rhineland in 1936? [2 marks]

2. What, do you think, did Lord Lothian mean when he said that the Germans were 'going into their own back garden'? [4 marks]

Source C

'Neither the British nor the French people were prepared to go to war to prevent German Austria from becoming a part of the German Reich. Indeed, there were many who believed that Austria, in the truncated form to which it had been reduced by the Treaty of Versailles, could not exist as an independent state.'

Lord Templewood: *Nine Troubled Years* (1954)

(Lord Templewood was a member of the British cabinet in 1938)

Specimen question

Lord Templewood's account of why Britain and France allowed Hitler to take over Austria in 1938 was written many years after the event. Do you think it is reliable? Explain your answer.

[5 marks]

Hint

Notice the position Templewood held in 1938.

Model answer

As a member of the British cabinet which decided not to oppose Hitler, Templewood would want to show that the decision was justified. It is probably true that the British people opposed risking war to stop Hitler, but the idea that many people thought that Austria was too small to survive is difficult to prove. He does not say, even though it is true, that some ministers believed that Hitler was right to take over Austria. So the account is only partly reliable.

Source D

ANGLO-FRENCH SECURITY

FRENCH ALLIANCES

RUMANIA

POLAND

CZECHO

NEWS

LOW

WHAT'S CZECHOSLOVAKIA TO ME, ANYWAY ?

A cartoon drawn by David Low in 1938

Source E

'Czechoslovakia had a very weak moral and practical case in the matter of Sudetenland. [Fair-minded people] ... condemned that portion of the Peace Treaty which placed millions of Germans under Polish, Italian and Czech rule.'

Lord Winterton: *Orders of the Day* (1953)

(Lord Winterton was a member of the British cabinet in 1938)

Source F

'Had Czechoslovakia defended herself we would have been held up by fortifications in the east, for we did not have the means to break through.'

Erich Von Manstein, German general, speaking in 1946

Source G

'The year of respite from war which Munich afforded was perhaps the most valuable in our history for the defence of these islands. Without it, we should not have had the Hurricanes and Spitfires to win the Battle of Britain.'

Lord Winterton: *Orders of the Day* (1953)

Specimen question

(a) Did David Low, who drew the cartoon, agree with the attitude of the man in the deckchair? Explain your answer. [4 marks]

(b) Both Lord Winterton and the character in the cartoon were against interfering to protect Czechoslovakia. How did their reasons differ? [5 marks]

2

Specimen question

Read Sources F and G.

(a) To what extent do they contradict each other?

[4 marks]

(b) Which do you consider the more reliable? Explain your answer. [6 marks]

Model answer

(a) Sources F and G completely contradict each other. Winterton takes it for granted that in 1938 Britain, allied with Czechoslovakia, would not have been strong enough to go to war against Germany, while Manstein says that in 1938 Germany would not have been strong enough to defeat just Czechoslovakia.

(b) Von Manstein is probably more reliable. Winterton, a member of Chamberlain's government in 1938, was trying to justify the decision not to help the Czechs, and in any case did not know as much as the German general Manstein about the strength of the German forces in 1938. Nor could he have been certain that, if war had broken out in 1938, a fight similar to the Battle of Britain would have taken place. Finally, Manstein had no reason not to tell the truth on this particular subject in 1946.

Specimen question

Is it fair to say that the main reason why France and Britain refused to act against Hitler before 1939 was that the 1919 treaty had treated Germany unfairly? Explain your answer fully.

[15 marks]

Hints

Remember to look for evidence *for* and *against* the view stated in the question. Sources B, C and E all contain evidence to support it, but Source G suggests that fear of the strength of Germany's forces played a part, while Source D shows that many people did not care. So perhaps the strictness of the treaty made people unwilling to enforce it, but indifference and fear of another war against Germany might have been just as important. Remember in History it is very difficult to be certain exactly *why* things happen.

The invasion of Poland

In the summer of 1939 Hitler was ready to attack Poland to win back the German land lost in the 1919 treaty. Britain and France had promised to support Poland if this happened. Hitler was ready to run this risk. But he feared that the Soviet Union, who had once owned much of Poland, might oppose him. So he began to negotiate with the Soviet government, and on 21 August the two countries signed a non-aggression pact, which contained a secret clause dividing Poland between them.

On 1 September German troops invaded Poland. Britain and France demanded that they withdraw. Hitler refused, so on 3 September 1939 France and Britain declared war on Germany.

Source A

'*Everything I undertake is directed against Russia. If the West is too stupid and too blind to understand that I will be forced to come to an understanding with the Russians, to smash the West and then ... to turn against the Soviet Union.*'

Hitler in conversation, 11 August 1939

Source B

'We knew that Hitler was trying to trick us with the treaty. I heard with my own ears Stalin say that because of this treaty the war would pass us by for a while longer. We would be able to stay neutral and save our strength.'

Nikita Khrushchev: *Khrushchev on Khrushchev* (1960)

(Khrushchev was a member of the Soviet government in 1939)

Specimen questions

1 Do you think Hitler was speaking the truth in Source A? Explain your answer. [4 marks]

Hint

Remember that Hitler was a great talker, who liked to impress or even shock his listeners and was therefore likely to exaggerate. But also remember his plans for *lebensraum* and what in fact happened in the war.

2 What did Hitler and Stalin gain from the Nazi–Soviet pact? [4 marks]

Background to the Nazi–Soviet pact

The alliance between Hitler and the USSR might not have happened.

Source A

'My general impression is that the Soviet Government are at present determined to conclude an agreement with Britain and France if they fulfil all Soviet wishes.'

Schulenburg (German ambassador to Moscow): Dispatch to Berlin, 4 August 1939

Source B

'If we are going in [to promise to help Poland] without the help of Russia we are walking into a trap. It is the only country whose arms can get there.'

Lloyd George: House of Commons speech, April 1939

Source C

'Chamberlain [Britain's Prime Minister] never wanted association with the Soviet Union except on impossible terms.'

A J P Taylor: *The Origins of the Second World War* (1961)

Specimen question

What evidence is there in the source that Britain, France and the USSR might have made a treaty if Chamberlain had not been Prime Minister? Explain your answer. [6 marks]

check

that you understand how Hitler's policies led to war in 1939.

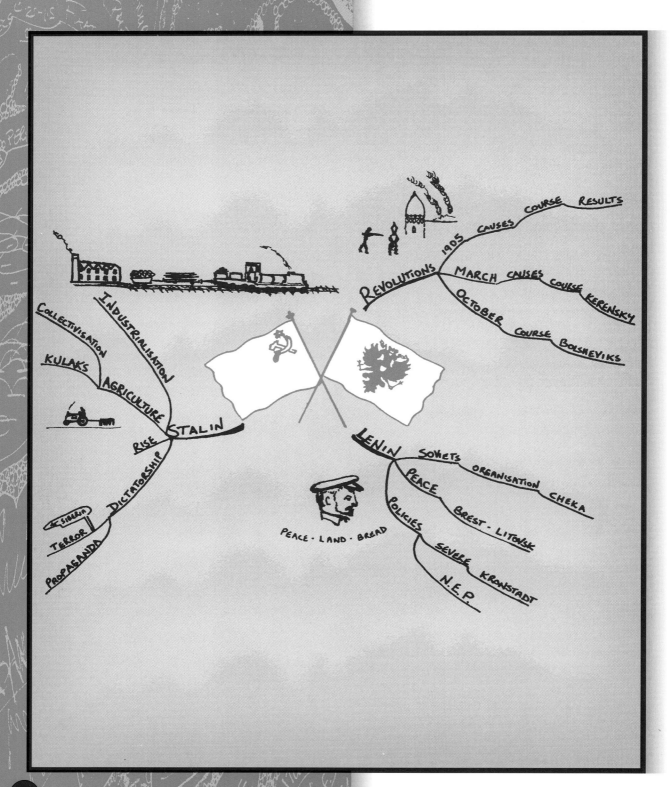

preview
What you need to know

- **Why a revolution broke out in 1905, how the Czar dealt with it, and what followed**

- **Why a revolution took place in March 1917, and what followed it**

- **How the Bolsheviks seized power in October 1917**

- **The system of government set up by Lenin, the civil war which followed the revolution, and Lenin's policies**

- **How Stalin came to power and how he used it**

A note on dates

Until 1918 the Russian calendar was 13 days behind the rest of Europe. The dates in this chapter all use the new system.

Location of Port Arthur

The 1905 Revolution

Causes

In 1904 war broke out between Japan and Russia. In December 1904 the Japanese captured the Russian naval base of Port Arthur. In January 1905 a revolution broke out in Russia.

Source A

'What little my parents earned was spent on bread. Thanks to the neighbours we were sometimes given porridge or cabbage soup. This was the usual tradition amongst the peasants of Russia, who all knew what it was like to live in great need.'

Marshall Georgi Zhukov: *Memories and Reflections* (1965)

Source B

'Coal, iron, oil and textile industries all existed.... Most of these workers lived in wretched poverty, inhabiting poor homes and working long hours.'

S H Wood: *World Affairs 1900 to the Present Day* (1970)

Specimen question

Give three possible causes of the 1905 revolution in Russia. Explain your answer.   [5 marks]

Hint

The sources and the introduction give you all the information you need. Why was it likely that many people would want to get rid of the government in Russia in 1905?

The events of the Revolution

1905 Revolution timetable

22 January	(Bloody Sunday) Troops in St Petersburg fired on a peaceful demonstration.
28 June	Crew of Battleship *Potemkin* mutinied.
October	General strike all over western Russia. Czar promised an elected '*Duma*' (Parliament) with a Prime Minister. This split the Revolutionaries. Then the Czar restored order.

Source A

'Now at last my people and I are at peace,' says the Tsar.

This cartoon appeared in a Russian magazine in 1906

Source B

'*By the time the Czar was compelled to summon the first Duma in April 1906 it is estimated that his government had killed some 15,000 people and arrested 70,000.*'

David Thomson: *Europe Since Napoleon* (1966)

Specimen questions

1 How did the Czar's government restore order? [3 marks]

2 Did the author of Source A approve or disapprove of the Czar's actions? Explain your answer. [5 marks]

Hint

You need to explain how the cartoonist made his feelings clear in his drawing.

3 To what extent does the author of Source B confirm the impression given by Source A? [3 marks]

The Dumas

The Mind Map shows you by whom the Duma was elected and what its powers were.

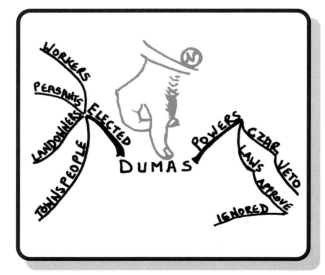

Duma timetable

First Duma **May–July 1906**	Dissolved – too critical of Czar.
Second Duma **March–June 1907**	Dissolved – too critical of Czar.
(Electoral system then altered, giving more power to the upper classes.)	
Third Duma **1907–12**	Uncritical – ran full term.
Fourth Duma **1912–17**	Criticised war policy. Czar dissolved it.

Notice how much information can be crammed into a table. Compile your own to help your revision.

Source A

'In my mind his Majesty the Emperor is the anointed of God ... When the will of such a man is made clear ... loyal subjects must submit, no matter what the consequences.'

I Goremykin, Prime Minister of Russia: Speech, 1906

Source B

'Let it be known that I, devoting all my strength to the pursuit of the good of my people, will maintain the principle of autocracy.'

Czar Nicholas II: Speech, 1894

Source C

'The Duma ... retained the right to examine the greater part of the budget. Every Minister, therefore, ... was bound to seek its goodwill.'

Sir Bernard Pares: A History of Russia (1947)

Specimen question

Why was Czar Nicholas II unable to work with the Dumas between 1906 and 1914? Explain your answer. [6 marks]

Hint

Note that the Czar believed in 'autocracy' – that is one person having complete control. Notice, too, the attitude of his Prime Minister. How do these match up with the idea that the Duma had the 'right', for instance, to examine the budget?

check

that you can explain why revolution occurred in 1905, how the Czar dealt with it, and how it affected the government of Russia.

3

The March Revolution

In August 1914 the First World War began, and the Russian army was mobilised and went to war. By the middle of September they had been defeated in two battles, at Tannenberg and the Masurian Lakes and had lost more than 200,000 men. In 1915 the Czar took personal control of the army.

Source A

'[In 1914] troops were embarking for the front. A packed train was on the point of leaving. Inside the young faces of the soldiers were cheerful. They were singing rousing marching songs … A wave of fervent patriotism swept over Russia.'

Eugenie Fraser: *The House by the Dvina* (1984)

(Eugenie Fraser lived in Russia until 1920. In 1984 she wrote her memoirs, *The House by the Dvina*)

Source B

In 1916 a wounded soldier visited Eugenie Fraser's home. He said:

'Some of us were defending mother Russia with our bare hands – lucky to lift a rifle from a dead comrade … I've had enough, the stink of death, the rotting bodies, flies, maggots – and all for what? For nothing … Russia is finished.'

Source C

Facts and figures				
	1914	**1915**	**1916**	**1917**
Prices (%)	100	125	130	400
Bread ration		2.5 lb	2 lb	1.5 lb
Size of army	5.5 m	10 m	15 m	36 m

Source D

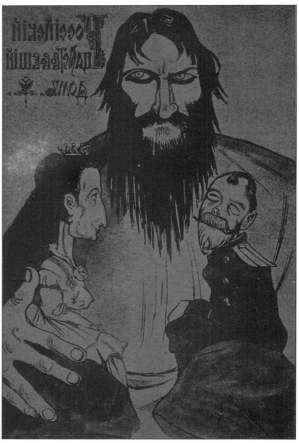

A contemporary cartoon, showing Rasputin

Source E

'Everybody was fed up with the Czar because they thought he was weak.... He was much criticised. There were lots of scandals at court.'

Margot Tracey, daughter of a wealthy businessman living in Russia at the time: Television interview, 1990

Source F

'Don't yield. Be the boss. Obey your firm little wife and Our Friend [Rasputin]. Believe in us.'

Letter from Czarina to Nicholas II, 1916

March 1917 Revolution timetable

8 March   Strikes in Petrograd, protesting against food shortages. Mutinies in the army.

12 March   Workers and soldiers in Petrograd elected a 'soviet' (committee) to represent them. The Czar's ministers fled.

15 March   Nicholas II, trapped in his train on his way to Petrograd, met delegates from the Duma and a number of generals. All advised him to abdicate. He did, and power passed to the leaders of the Duma and the Soviet.

Specimen questions

1   Was Nicholas II to blame for the 1917 March Revolution? Explain your answer fully, using both the sources and your own knowledge.

[15 marks]

Hints

Always be suspicious of one simple explanation for events. But beware of just listing the causes of the revolution. To get really good marks you need to use the sources to back up your opinion of how far Nicholas was to blame.

Model answer

In theory, Nicholas was to blame because he had been in sole charge of Russia since 1894. But, in fact, some of the problems were not entirely his fault.

The army's lack of equipment which angered soldiers (Source B) after they had been so patriotic in 1914 (Source A) was due to Russia's inefficient industry and administration. These would have been difficult for Nicholas to correct, and he could not be blamed for short rations and high prices in Petrograd, which were partly caused by the number of peasants taken off the land to serve in the army (Source C). After all, Nicholas was away with the army.

But he *was* to blame for allowing the unpopular (Source D) and scandalous (Source E) Rasputin too much influence. Source E says that people thought Nicholas was weak. This view is backed up by Source F, which shows that the Czarina thought he needed firm encouragement.

The feeling that a weak man was in charge at such a time must have encouraged people to get rid of him. So, though Nicholas could not be directly blamed for the immediate causes of the revolution, his character and some of his actions made it much more likely.

Now, using the same sources and your own knowledge, try to answer question 2.

2   Do you agree that the 1917 March Revolution was caused by the grievances of the workers? Explain your answer fully.   [15 marks]

3

The provisional government

A new provisional government, headed by a nobleman, Prince Lvov, replaced the Czar.

Source A

'[The Government's] orders are executed only insofar as this is permitted by the Soviet of Workers' and Soldiers' Deputies which holds in its hands the most important elements of actual power, such as troops, railways, postal and telegraph services.'

A L Guchov, Defence Minister, in a letter, April 1917

Source B

'Lynch law, the destruction of houses and shops … unauthorised arrests, seizures and beatings-up were recorded every day by tens and hundreds … The soldiers, without leave, went off home in great floods.'

N Sukhanov, a Menshevik leader: *Memoirs* (1955)

Source C

'When [the government] promise you a lot they are deceiving you and the whole Russian people. The people needs peace; the people needs bread; the people needs land. And they give war, hunger, no bread – leave the landlords still in the land.'

V Lenin: Speech, April 1917

Specimen questions

1 Which do you think had more power after the March Revolution – the Soviet or the provisional government? Explain your answer. [4 marks]

2 What evidence is there that the provisional government could not:
(a) control the army,
(b) enforce law and order? [3 marks]

3 Do you think Lenin's criticism of the provisional government was fair? Explain your answer. [4 marks]

Hint

Remember, when answering question 3, that the government was provisional and temporary.

check

that you understand why a revolution happened in March 1917 and why the provisional government which followed it was so weak.

The Bolshevik Revolution

In 1903 there was a meeting of the Russian Social Democratic Party in London. The Party split. The majority (in Russian the Bolshevik) wanted violent revolution. The minority (in Russian the Menshevik) wanted gradual change.

By the middle of 1917 the Bolsheviks, led by Lenin and Trotsky (a former Menshevik), had seized control of the Russian government from the democratic Prime Minister, Kerensky. How were they able to do this?

Source A

'Either we must abandon our slogan "All power to the Soviets", or else we must make an insurrection. There is no middle course.'

V Lenin: Speech, 31 October 1917

All power to the Soviets
Immediate truce on all fronts
Landlord estates ... to the peasants
Workers' control over industrial production
An ... honestly elected Constituent Assembly

Demands published in *Rabochi i Soldat*, a Bolshevik newspaper, 17 October 1917

Source C

'The inflated puppets of the Winter Palace understood nothing. Thinking themselves strong, they felt no alarm ... They told each other that steps had been and would be taken ... and [did] nothing else.'

N K Sukhanov, a socialist journalist, writing in his memoirs (1955) about the provisional government

Specimen question

Read the timetable and the sources. What evidence is there in them that:

1 Trotsky was a good organiser and a clever plotter;

2 The Bolsheviks had policies which would appeal to many peasants, soldiers and industrial workers;

3 Lenin was a clear and decisive leader;

4 The provisional government was weak and indecisive?

[15 marks]

check

Design your own Mind Map showing why the 1917 Bolshevik Revolution succeeded.

October Revolution timetable

September	General Kornilov tried to overthrow Kerensky. The Bolsheviks helped to defeat him and took control of the Petrograd Soviet.
12 October	Petrograd Soviet appointed a military committee under Trotsky to 'defend the revolution'.
25 October	Trotsky obtained 5,000 rifles to equip a 'Red Army of workers'.
3 November	Trotsky appointed a Soviet commissar to liaise with every regiment in Petrograd. Told the troops to obey the commissar, not their officers.
5 November	Trotsky distributed arms and ordered troops to take over strong points in the city. Kerensky ordered his arrest and that of Lenin.
7 November	Kerensky left Petrograd. All-Russian Congress of Soviets, called by the Petrograd Soviet, took charge.
8 November	Bolsheviks captured the Winter Palace.
13 November	Bolshevik army defeated Kerensky's forces. Kerensky fled abroad.

3

Lenin's government

The Soviet system

The Bolsheviks set up a new system of government dominated by the Communist Party.

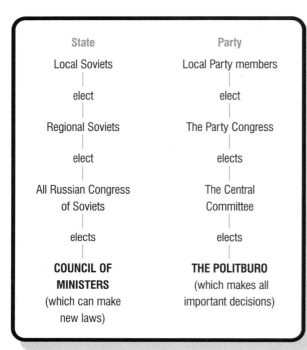

State	Party
Local Soviets	Local Party members
elect	elect
Regional Soviets	The Party Congress
elect	elects
All Russian Congress of Soviets	The Central Committee
elects	elects
COUNCIL OF MINISTERS (which can make new laws)	**THE POLITBURO** (which makes all important decisions)

Only people approved by the Communist Party could stand for office. They called the new state the Union of Soviet Socialist Republics (USSR).

Specimen question

Supporters of the Soviet Union claimed that the Soviet system was democratic. Opponents said it was not. How could both have justified their views? [3 marks]

The Cheka

The Bolsheviks set up a secret police – the Cheka – to enforce their policies.

'The Cheka is the defence of the revolution … as the Red Army cannot stop to ask whether it may harm particular individuals … so the Cheka must … conquer the enemy even if its sword falls occasionally on the heads of the innocent.'

The Head of the Cheka at a press conference in 1918

Source B

'People we knew vanished from the face of the earth. Those living near the outskirts of the town saw, in the early hours of the morning, prisoners taken by the back streets to the woods, and heard the sounds of shots as they were summarily executed.'

Eugenie Fraser: *The House by the Dvina* (memoirs) (1984)

Specimen questions

1 Eugenie Fraser's family were industrialists in Archangel. Does this make her account more or less likely to be true? Explain your answer. [5 marks]

Hints

Was she an eye-witness of the events she describes? Was she likely to approve of the revolution? Might she have checked carefully on stories of mysterious shootings at the time, or exaggerated them as the years passed?

2 Does the statement by the head of the Cheka make you more or less likely to believe Eugenie Fraser's account. Explain your answer. [4 marks]

check

that you understand the Soviet system of government.

The Treaty of Brest Litovsk

In December 1917 Trotsky began to negotiate with the German government for a peace treaty. In March 1918 they signed the Treaty of Brest Litovsk.

Source A

This map shows the land lost by the USSR by the Treaty of Brest Litovsk

Source B

'Our impulse tells us to refuse to sign this robber peace.'

V Lenin, March 1918

Specimen question

Does Source A confirm Lenin's view that Brest Litovsk was a 'robber peace'? Explain your answer. [5 marks]

Hints

Notice the huge area lost by Russia. But remember the Bolsheviks' slogans about the need for peace. Remember the political systems in Germany and Russia. Were the Germans justified in taking all they could?

check

that you can explain the terms of the Treaty of Brest Litovsk.

The Civil War 1918–22

After the Revolution the Bolshevik government had to fight a civil war which they finally won in 1922. Their opponents were known as the 'Whites'. The Mind Map below and the annotated map of the USSR on the next page will remind you of the main events and issues.

North
French and British troops went to help White Russians July 1918 to October 1919.

Murmansk

Archangel

Petrograd

Moscow

Kazan

Odessa

Siberia
Czech ex prisoners of war helped by US and Japanese troops fought against the Bolsheviks 1918–1922.

Ukraine
White forces were helped by troops from Poland, which wanted to take over Ukraine. Defeated in 1921.

Ekaterinburg
The fighting alarmed the commissar in charge of Czar and his family. So he had them shot.

Batum

Black Sea

Baku

Caspian Sea

South
White forces were helped by France and Britain. Defeated by November 1920.

The main events of the Civil War

Maps combined with notes can hold a lot of information. Draw your own to help with your revision.

Source A

'Every grain collection squad must have at least 75 men with two or three machine guns.'

Instruction to grain collection squads, August 1918

Source B

'The workers of the towns and some of the villages choke in the throes of hunger. The railroads barely crawl. The houses are crumbling. The towns are full of refuse. Epidemics spread and death strikes to the right and to the left. Industry is ruined.'

Pravda (Communist Party newspaper), 26 February 1920

Specimen question

Use the Mind Map and the annotated map to find out:

1 Two advantages which helped the Reds to win;

2 Two disadvantages which led the Whites to lose;

3 Three countries which helped the Whites. Suggest reasons why they may have done so. **[10 marks]**

War Communism

The Soviet government had handed land over to the peasants, and factories to the workers. They allowed peasants to keep enough food for their families, and ordered them to hand over the rest to the state.

Specimen question

Suggest two reasons why the grain collection squads had to be armed. **[3 marks]**

Hint

Think of the attitude of the peasants and the general shortage of food.

Source C

'Workers and peasants are so enfeebled that they are almost incapable of work.'

V Lenin: Speech to 1921 Communist Party Congress

Specimen question

In 1921 sailors at the Baltic naval base of Kronstadt rebelled against the Soviet government. Use the sources and your own knowledge to explain why they did so. [10 marks]

Hints

The Soviet government had promised to improve life for the Russian people. Had it done so? If not, in what ways was life worse? How might this have made the sailors at Kronstadt decide to try to overthrow the government?

The New Economic Policy

Lenin decided that War Communism was not working. So he introduced a new economic policy. The Mind Map shows its main features.

Production of goods and foodstuffs increased. But in 1923 they were still below 1914 levels. In 1924 Lenin died.

In 1925 Maynard Keynes, a British economist, visited the USSR.

Source D

'So, now the deeds are done and there is no going back … Even allowing for everything, if I were a Russian … I [would rather] contribute my quota of activity to Soviet Russia than to Czarist Russia.'

J M Keynes: *A Short View of Russia* (1925)

Specimen questions

1. What actions taken by Lenin and the Bolsheviks may Keynes have been thinking of when he says 'even allowing for everything'? [4 marks]

2. What examples of life in Russia before and after the Revolution might Keynes have given in 1925 to support his judgement? [6 marks]

check

that you can explain how War Communism and the New Economic Policy differed.

3

Stalin and the USSR

Stalin comes to power

There were at least four men who might have taken power in the USSR on Lenin's death in 1924. They were Trotsky, Kamanev, Zinoviev and Stalin, who was General Secretary of the Soviet Communist Party. Lenin left a will, which mentioned Stalin.

Source

'Stalin, having become General Secretary, has concentrated enormous power in his hands … I propose that the comrades find a way to remove Stalin from the position and appoint another man, loyal, more courteous, more considerate, etc.'

V Lenin: *Will*

Specimen questions

1 What weaknesses did Lenin see in Stalin? [2 marks]

2 Lenin's will was read out to the Party Central Committee. Many expected it to be published. What effect would this have had on Stalin's chance of being elected leader? [2 marks]

Stalin's tactics

Many people thought that Trotsky, still in charge of the Red Army, should be the new leader, but some long-serving Bolsheviks did not trust him because he joined the Bolsheviks only in 1917. So when Stalin offered to help Kamanev and Zinoviev to defeat Trotsky they willingly agreed. In return they agreed to help Stalin to suppress Lenin's will. So it was never published.

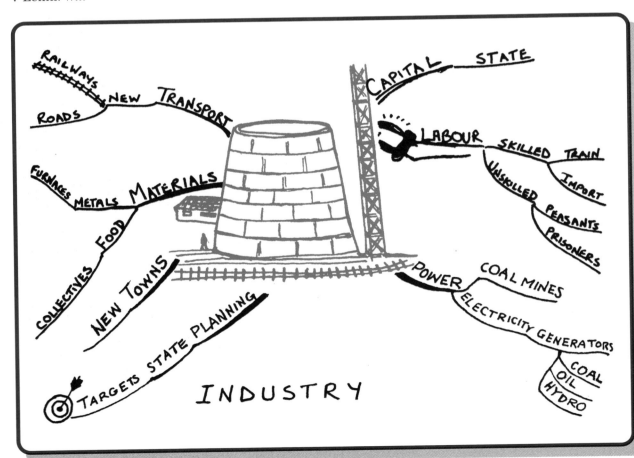

Meanwhile Stalin, Kamenev and Zinoviev persuaded the Central Committee to put Trotsky in charge of the electrification of the USSR. This meant he had to resign as Commander in Chief of the Red Army, which was the basis of his power. All the while, Stalin was using his position as General Secretary to increase his support on the Central Committee.

When he was ready he turned on Kamenev and Zinoviev. His supporters voted them and Trotsky off the Politburo and the Central Committee. Then in 1927 they were voted out of the Party. By 1928 Stalin was in complete control.

Specimen question

Read the account of how Stalin got to power. Would his methods have inspired affection, respect, or fear? Explain your answer. [5 marks]

check

that you understand how Stalin came to power.

Stalin's industrial policies

Stalin wanted to turn the USSR into a great industrial power and he instituted a Five Year Plan to achieve this. The Mind Map will remind you of what industry needs to grow, and how Stalin provided it.

Source A

'We are 50 or 100 years behind the advanced countries. We must make good the lag in ten years. Either we do it or they will crush us.'

Stalin: Speech, 1931

Specimen questions

1 Why did Stalin think it vital for the USSR to catch up quickly? [2 marks]

2 Did he prove to be right? Explain your answer. [4 marks]

Source B

'How was it possible at one of the most difficult times to raise these great construction sites? It was only possible through the unity of the people and the love of the people for their idol, because for us Stalin was an idol.'

Tatiana Fedorova, 1930s construction worker: Documentary film, 1995

Source C

A Soviet propaganda poster, published in 1931

3

Source D

'In early April it was still bitter cold, everything was frozen solid. By May the city was swimming in mud. Bubonic Plague had broken out not far from Magnitogorsk. The resistance of the population was very low because of under nourishment and consistent overwork. Sanitary conditions were appalling ... We were consumed by bed bugs and other vermin.'

John Scott: *Behind the Urals* (1942)

(John Scott was an American welder, working on the new town of Magnitogorsk)

Specimen questions

1 Source C is a 1931 poster designed to attract women to work in industrial centres. To what extent is its message contradicted by the information in Source D? Which is more reliable? Explain your answer. [6 marks]

2 Was Tatiana Fedorova (Source B) right to think that the construction sites were built because of the 'unity of the people' inspired by their 'idol' Stalin? Explain your answer. [10 marks]

Hints

What about fear, orders from the top, foreign help (e.g. John Scott), forced labour, etc?

The results of industrialisation

Source A

Production (millions of tons)		
	1929	1940
Coal	40	164
Iron and steel	9	36
Oil	13	34
(Soviet statistics)		

Source B

'1938 [Magnitogorsk] ... did boast 50 schools, 3 colleges, 2 large theatres, half a dozen small ones, 17 libraries, 22 clubs, 18 clinics ... A large park had been constructed in 1935.'

John Scott: *Behind the Urals* (1942)

Specimen questions

1 Does Source A prove that Stalin's industrial policy was a success? Explain your answer. [6 marks]

Hints

Remember that it is difficult to prove most things. Consider what happened to production. Is this what Stalin wanted? Might other methods have worked better? Are the figures reliable? Come to a conclusion.

2 How does Source B support the view that Stalin had the interests of Soviet workers at heart? [3 marks]

check

that you understand the changes Stalin wanted to make in Russia's industry and how far he achieved them.

The collectivisation of agriculture

Industrial towns needed a reliable supply of food. Lenin's New Economic Policy did not provide it because the peasants could decide how much they would sell to the state. In addition, peasants with their small farms could not afford to improve their land or buy the latest machinery. So they produced very little to send to the towns.

Source A

'The way out is to unite the small and dwarf peasant farms gradually but surely, not by pressure but by example and persuasion into large farms based on the common co-operative cultivation of the land. There is no other way out.'

Stalin: Speech to Communist Party Congress, 1927

Source B

'We have passed to the policy of eliminating the kulaks as a class … We must strike at the kulaks, strike so hard as to prevent them rising to their feet again. We must annihilate them as a social class.'

Stalin: Speech to Communist Party Congress, 1929

Specimen questions

1   Read Source A. How did Stalin intend to overcome the problem of low food production?   [3 marks]

2   Did Stalin expect serious opposition to his policy? Explain your answer.   [8 marks]

Model answer

Stalin must have known that peasants who had been given their land as a result of the Bolshevik Revolution would not want to hand it over to a collective farm. But in 1927 he seemed to think that the holders of 'small and dwarf plots' could be persuaded to give up their land by gradual, peaceful methods. By 1929 he was convinced that the *kulaks*, rich peasants who had more to lose, would never be persuaded. He thought the only way to get their land was to annihilate them as a social class. So he expected little opposition from poor peasants, but determined opposition from the kulaks.

Source C

'The majority of kulaks were deported to uninhabited areas in the East. There they were left … homeless, without food, tools or seed. The great majority died from starvation, disease and exposure.'

E M Roberts: *Stalin: man of steel* (1968)

Specimen question

What does the fate of the kulaks tell us about Stalin's character?   [3 marks]

Collectivisation in action

Stalin altered the system of collecting food from the peasants. Officials decided how much each collective had to contribute, and allowed the peasants to keep only what was left.

Source A

'Both those who joined the collective and the individual farmers killed their stock. Bulls, sheep, pigs, even cows were slaughtered, as well as cattle for breeding. "Kill, it's not ours any more … Kill, they will take it for meat anyway."'

M Sholokov: *Virgin Soil Upturned* (a novel) (1940)

Source B

An official photograph of peasants queuing to join a collective

Source C

'We've eaten everything we could lay our hands on – cats, dogs, field mice, birds … You will see that the trees have been stripped of their bark, for that too has been eaten. And the horse manure has been eaten, we fight over it. Sometimes there are whole grains in it.'

A peasant in the village of Petrovo, reporting to Viktor Kravchenko, a party worker sent to collect the grain quota

Source D

Agricultural statistics				
	Grain (millions of tons)		Livestock (millions)	
	Harvest	To towns	Pigs	Cattle
1928	73	11	26	60
1930	83	22		
1932	70	19		
1934	68	26	12	30

Notes

In the grain table the figures under 'Harvest' give the total grain harvest in millions of tons. The figures under 'To towns' give the amount sent to feed those living in the towns.

In the livestock table the figures give the total number of pigs and cattle in the USSR in the year in question.

Figures are only approximate.

Specimen questions

1 What impressions do (a) Source A, and (b) Source B give of the peasants' feelings about collectivisation? Explain your answers. [5 marks]

2 Do Sources C and D tend to support Source A or Source B? Explain your answer. [4 marks]

3 What do we have to take into account about (a) Source A, (b) Source B, and (c) Source C when trying to decided how reliable each of them is? [6 marks]

Hints

Who wrote/produced/said them? What impressions might they have been trying to make?

4 Did collectivisation fulfil Stalin's aims? Explain your answer. [10 marks]

Hints

Look at the figures in Source D. What happened to food production? Would this have pleased Stalin? What happened to the amount of food going to the towns? Would this have pleased Stalin? Who suffered as a result of collectivisation? Would Stalin have cared? Evidence for this?

check

that you understand why Stalin wanted collectivisation, how it was imposed, and what the effects were.

Stalin in power

Stalin controlled every aspect of Soviet life (*see* the Mind Map). He used his control over the media and the system of justice to maintain his hold on power.

Source A

'We live so well. Our hearts are so joyful. In no other country are there such happy young people as us … and on behalf of all young people I want to thank our party and our dear comrade Stalin for this joy we have.'

Tatiana Fedorova in a 1932 Soviet propaganda film

Specimen questions

1 What was the aim of the piece of soundtrack spoken by Tatiana Fedorova in 1932? [2 marks]

2 Which young people in the USSR would probably not have had 'joyful hearts' in 1932? Explain your answer. [4 marks]

3 Study the Mind Map, and Source A on page 54. Compare them with Sources A and B on page 41. In what ways was the position of Stalin **(a)** similar to, and **(b)** different from that of Czar Nicholas? [5 marks]

Hints

Uncritical admiration? Determination to retain power? Role of religion.

Silencing opposition

After 1934 Stalin used mass arrests, show trials, executions and deportations to labour camps to get rid of his opponents. Between 1934 and 1941, 30 million were arrested, of whom about 16 million died or were executed.

Source A

'Thousands and thousands of corpses were buried in more than 500 mass graves. The massacres were carried out over four years from 1937 … Residents … could not sleep at night for the sound of machine guns … The victims covered all professions, from engineers and teachers to soldiers and communist party workers. They were all branded under the common term "enemy of the people" and shot by the NKVD.'

Alex Adamovitch, Byelorussian journalist, quoted in *The Guardian*, 26 September 1988

Source B

'Before dawn we were marched to a bleak open field. Until 1 pm we hacked at the frozen soil with spades. We ate between 1 pm and 1.30 at the camp, trying to warm ourselves over the stove. From 1.30 pm until 8 pm we worked again.'

Eugenia Ginzberg (18 years a political prisoner): *Into the Whirlwind* (1981)

Source C

'When he said, "You can't imagine it, Stalin is shooting all the present members of the Politburo!", and he counted them off one by one, I couldn't bear it. We were having lunch. I picked up a knife and threw it at him.'

Ella Shistyer, speaking of her first husband in a 1995 documentary. He was later killed by the secret police. Ella was later imprisoned in Siberia.

Source D

'What would you have said in my place if you had heard a man confess his crimes with your own ears?'

Boris Yeminov, a political cartoonist who attended the 1930s treason trials, in a 1995 documentary

Specimen questions

1 Are Sources A and B good evidence that Stalin was using terror tactics against his opponents between 1934 and 1941? [6 marks]

2 Why did Ella Shistyer find it so hard to accept her husband's accusations against Stalin? Refer to Source D and use your own knowledge. [4 marks]

Hint

Think about the power of propaganda.

check

that you understand the methods which Stalin used to stay in power.

Conclusion

In 1941 Hitler invaded the USSR. It held out against his forces and in the end defeated them. Here are two views of Stalin's work.

Source A

'He was the greatest enemy of Socialism. He had damaged Socialism by destroying people in all parts of life, in agriculture, the arts, the military, the party. He destroyed people everywhere. Wasn't that evil?'

Mikhail Mindlin, a political prisoner 1937–54, in a 1995 documentary

Source B

'As I think back, I ask myself, again and again: was there an alternative to the indiscriminate, brutal, basically unplanned rush forward of the first Five Year Plan? I wish I could say there was, but I cannot. I cannot find an answer.'

Oskar Lange, a socialist economist, quoted by Eric Hobsbawm in *Age of Extremes* (1994)

Specimen question

Should the Soviet union have been grateful to Stalin? Explain your answer fully. [15 marks]

Hints

This question needs you to strike a balance. What did Stalin do that was good for the Soviet Union, and what did he do that damaged it, and which outweighed the other? You should consider the way he built up Soviet industry. Could the USSR have been strong enough to resist Germany in 1941 without his work? On the other hand, what was his effect on Soviet agriculture and on political life in the USSR? Come to a conclusion. Use the sources and the information in this section to help you.

4

The United States of America 1918–41

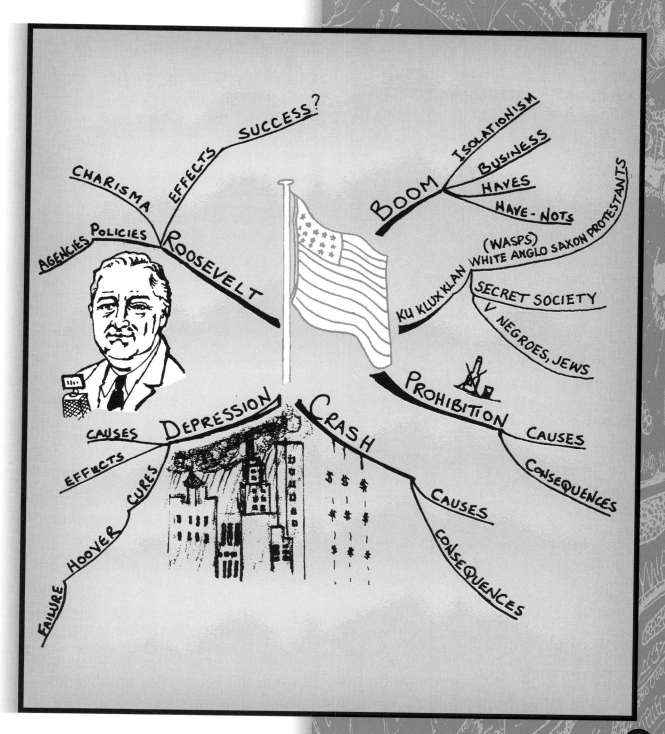

preview
What you need to know

- **American Society between 1918 and 1929, when sections of it were very prosperous**

- **Why the US government banned alcoholic drinks and what the results were**

- **Why the price of American stocks and shares rose, and then suddenly fell in October 1929, and what the results were**

- **Why the Great Depression happened, and how it affected American Society**

- **How President Roosevelt tackled the Great Depression**

- **The rise and decline of the Ku Klux Klan between 1915 and 1929**

The boom years

Isolationism

In 1918 the USA was the richest and most powerful country on Earth. Woodrow Wilson was President. He belonged to the Democratic Party. He had been elected in 1912 and re-elected in 1916. He had taken the USA into the First World War, helped to found the League of Nations, and wanted the USA to play a leading part in world politics.

The other main party was called the Republicans. They disagreed with Wilson.

Source

A typical Republican supporter, portrayed in a novel, said,

'What the country needs ... is [not] a lot of monkeying about with foreign affairs, but a good, sound, economical business administration that will give us a chance to have something like a decent turnover.'

Sinclair Lewis: *Babbitt* (1922)

Specimen question

Who and what was Babbitt probably thinking of when he talked about 'monkeying about with foreign affairs'?   [3 marks]

Republicans win control

In the 1918 elections the Republicans won control of the Senate and the House of Representatives. They reversed Wilson's policy. They refused to confirm the Treaty of Versailles and would not allow the USA to join the League of Nations. In 1920 the American people showed that they approved this policy by electing a Republican president.

The vast majority of the US population were either immigrants themselves or descended from immigrants. Between 1900 and 1915 over 13 million had landed. But after 1918 there was no shortage of labour in the USA. So in 1924 and 1929 Congress passed two acts limiting the number of immigrants to 150,000 a year.

Source

'Give me your tired, your poor,
Your huddled masses yearning to breathe free ...
Send these, the homeless, tempest-tost to me.'

Emma Lazarus: Inscription on the Statue of Liberty, 1903

Specimen question

Why in 1929 might most of the world's people feel that the US government had betrayed them?

[3 marks]

Business America

Calvin Coolidge, President of the USA from 1923 to 1929, said *'the business of America is business'*. The US government helped business in various ways (*see* diagram).

Specimen question

Study the diagram. How would American businesses have benefited from these policies?

[8 marks]

Mass production

American businessmen, using mass production methods developed by Henry Ford to manufacture their goods, and hire purchase to sell them, set to work.

Source A

In his novels, Sinclair Lewis wrote about the businessmen at the time.

'[Everyone] in the city was hustling for hustling's sake. Men in motors were hustling to pass one another in hustling traffic … Men were hustling … to gallop across the pavement, to hurl themselves into the buildings, into hustling express elevators … Men who had made five thousand the year before last and ten thousand last year, were urging on nerve-yelping bodies and parched brains so that they might make twenty thousand this year.'

Sinclair Lewis: *Babbitt* (1922)

Source B

'We are a happy people – the statistics prove it. We have more cars, more bath tubs, oil furnaces, silk stockings, bank accounts than any other people on earth.'

Herbert Hoover (President 1929–33): Speech, 1929

Source C

Table 1 Rise in income 1923–9 (%)

	Workers' pay	Company profits	Shareholders' dividends
1923	100	100	100
1929	111	162	165

Note: This table shows the percentage rise in workers' pay, company profits and shareholders' dividends between 1923 and 1929. Workers' pay had gone up 11%, profits 62% and dividends 65%.

Table 2

	Surfaced roads (km)	Telephones	Radios	Cars
1919	620,000	13 million	60,000	9 million
1929	1 million	20 million	10 million	26 million

Specimen questions

1. In Source A, Sinclair Lewis writes of businessmen 'hustling'. Did he approve of this? Explain your answer.　　[4 marks]

Hint

Why did Lewis think people were hustling? What effect did he think it would have on them?

Model answer

Sinclair Lewis disapproved of hustling businessmen. He thought hustling was pointless, 'hustling for hustling's sake', or that its aim was only to increase the businessmen's income, in spite of the damage it was likely to do to their health – 'nerve-yelping bodies and parched brains'.

2. Read Sources B and C. Would President Hoover have agreed with Lewis? Explain your answer. How might he have used the statistics in Source C to justify his view?　　[4 marks]

3. Why might the figures in Table 2 have encouraged workers to buy shares in US companies?　　[3 marks]

check

that you understand how the USA turned its back on the world and concentrated on making money.

American high society

Source A

'On weekends his Rolls Royce became an omnibus, bearing parties to and from the city between nine in the morning and long past midnight … Every Friday five crates of oranges and lemons arrived from a fruiterer in New York … By seven o'clock the orchestra has arrived, no thin five piece affair, but a whole pitful … The cars from New York are parked five deep in the drive, and already the halls and salons and verandas are gaudy with primary colours and hair bobbed in strange new ways.'

F Scott Fitzgerald: *The Great Gatsby* (a novel) (1926)

Source B

'F Scott Fitzgerald's brittle, brilliant novels of the "jazz age" caught the flavour of contemporary life perfectly.'

R B Nye and J E Morpurgo: *A History of the United States* (1955)

Specimen questions

1. Why would Source A be useful to historians studying social life in the USA in the 1920s?　　[4 marks]

2. What conclusions might they draw from it about the life led by the rich?　　[6 marks]

Farmers

Compared with businessmen, American farmers were not so well off. Their standard of living was worse in the 1920s than in the war (*see* the Mind Map).

Notes

After the war the US government put duties on imports. This meant that other countries were unable or unwilling to buy food from the USA. So farmers could not export their produce and were worse off because they lost a lot of their former income.

Source A

US farm prices: 1919–28		
	Cotton (cents per lb)	Wheat ($ per bushel)
1919	35	2.20
1922	23	1.00
1925	20	1.40
1928	18	1.00

Source B

'For three quarters of a century Southern tenant farmers, white and black, had been very sad citizens, the victims of worn-out crops, living off a diet of corn, fat back pork, and no green vegetables … They were exhausted from the twin diseases of malnutrition: scurvy and pellagra.'

Alistair Cooke: *America* (1973)

Specimen questions

1 What evidence is there in Source A that farmers in the USA did not share the general prosperity of the country?   [3 marks]

2 What evidence is there in Sources A and B that Southern farmers were particularly badly off?   [4 marks]

Hint

Remember that cotton was a staple crop of many Southern states.

check

that you understand how unequal American society was.

Prohibition

In 1919 the US government prohibited the manufacture and sale of alcohol throughout the country. Why did they do this and what were the results?

Why Prohibition happened

Source A

'The drinking habits of most of my patrons appeared frightful ... intoxication to the point of senselessness – and this not once in a while but frequently or daily ... My unmarried patrons spent about 75% of their earnings on drink.'

New York saloon keeper: *McClure's Magazine* (1908)

Source B

Daddy's in There---

And Our Shoes and Stockings and Clothes and Food Are in There, Too, and They'll Never Come Out.
—*Chicago American.*

This cartoon was published in *Chicago America* at the beginning of the 20th century

Specimen questions

1. In what ways does Source B add to the evidence of the saloon keeper?   [3 marks]

2. Why might Sources A and B persuade people that Prohibition would be a good thing?
[5 marks]

Hints

Waste of time and money? Damage to health and family life? Remember to refer to the sources in your answer.

Prohibition in action

During Prohibition it was easy to make money manufacturing and selling illegal drink. Distillers of poor quality 'hooch' used cheap ingredients and charged high prices. And they paid no taxes. High profits attracted gangsters to the trade. The most famous, Al Capone, wiped out all his rivals and got control of the drink trade in the whole of Chicago. He made a fortune of $27 million.

In 1933 Prohibition was abolished.

Source A

'You can find stills in practically every other home. They make it, they drink it, they sell it ... You see children drunk. I have seen them drunk myself.'

Evidence from a Pennsylvania priest to a Senate committee

Source B

'There are more than 30,000 speakeasies [illegal drinking places] in New York compared with fewer than 15,000 saloons before Prohibition. They are a terrible menace ... Fights are common in them, provoked by the raw liquor they sell and the unavoidable absence of police supervision.'

Judge Tally of New York, 1926

New York City deaths from alcoholic poisoning	
1920	98
1925	687
1926	760

Specimen question

How might an opponent of Prohibition have used the career of Al Capone and the information in Sources A, B and C to argue that it should be abolished?   [10 marks]

How did Al Capone make his money? What evidence was there that Prohibition was turning ordinary families into criminals? Was drink more difficult to get than before? Was drinking better controlled? How was Prohibition affecting public health? Remember to back up your answer by referring to the sources.

check

that you understand why the US government introduced Prohibition and why they reversed the ban in 1933.

The Wall Street Crash

Beware: Share trading can be complex and technical. This explanation tries to keep it simple. Work your way through it carefully.

How the Crash happened

Between 1921 and 1929 the price of shares traded on the New York stock exchange in Wall Street rose (*see* the graph).

Buying shares seemed an easy way to make money. People borrowed money to buy shares. When the time came to pay it back, they sold the shares, which had gone up in price and used the profit they had made to buy more shares. The fact that so many people wanted to buy shares pushed their prices even higher.

Eventually, in October 1929, some dealers decided that prices were too high. So they sold their shares. Other

US stockmarkets

Shares bought for $50 in 1921 were worth over $200 by the middle of 1929

$

1921 1922 1923 1924 1925 1926 1927 1928 1929

dealers were unwilling to buy them, so their price fell. Almost everybody now wanted to sell their shares before the price fell even further. As a result prices fell faster than ever.

On 'Black Thursday' 24 October, nearly 13 million shares were sold, and $4 million were lost. On 'Black Tuesday' 29 October more than 16 million shares were sold and the losses totalled more than $10 million. People lost their faith in shares, so they continued to fall in value.

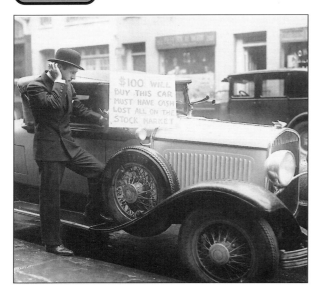

Results of the Crash

People who had borrowed money to buy shares could not pay it back when the shares lost their value. They went bankrupt. So did some of the banks which had lent them money. Other banks had less to lend.

The shortage of money affected everybody. They bought less. Factories produced less, and laid off workers. The workers bought even less, affecting other factories. The whole economy ran down (*see* the diagram).

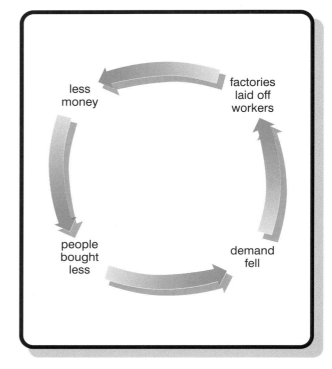

Specimen questions

Study Source A.

1. What date do you think the photograph was taken? Explain your answer. [3 marks]

2. Explain how the man in the photograph might have got into the position where he had to try to sell his car for $100? [5 marks]

check

that you understand the causes and results of the Wall Street Crash.

The Great Depression

The Wall Street Crash was followed by a slump in trade and industry which was so deep and so long lasting that it became known as the Great Depression.

Causes of the Depression

The most obvious cause of the Depression was the Wall Street Crash. But there were others. The Mind Map will help you to remember them.

Specimen question

Do you agree that the main cause of the Depression was the Wall Street Crash? Explain your answer fully. [15 marks]

Hints

Faced with a question like this, you have to decide what to put in, what to leave out and how to organise your answer. A couple of general rules:

1 You will not get good marks by discussing only the cause mentioned in the question. You need to deal with others as well.

2 Keep checking to make sure that you are answering the question. You get no credit for information, however accurate, that has nothing to do with the actual question.

Model answer

The American Depression was caused by a number of factors. The boom had to come to an end sooner or later. For one thing, by 1929 American factories were producing more than they could sell. So they would have had to cut production and lay off workers anyway. In addition, too much of the trade depended on borrowed money. Consumers used hire purchase to buy cars and household goods, and people who bought shares borrowed money to pay for them. Many owed more than they could afford to pay back, and so could not afford to buy more. So for this reason too, trade inevitably slowed down.

What was more, most Americans were not earning enough to keep the boom going. Farmers' incomes were less than in 1919, and workers' wages had not increased very much. So the boom was bound to end, even without the Crash. But the Crash made the Depression much worse than it need have been. It happened so suddenly that people had no time to adjust. Many people lost so much so quickly that they felt helpless. So the Wall Street Crash was not the main reason that the Depression happened, but it did make it worse.

check

that you understand why the Depression happened.

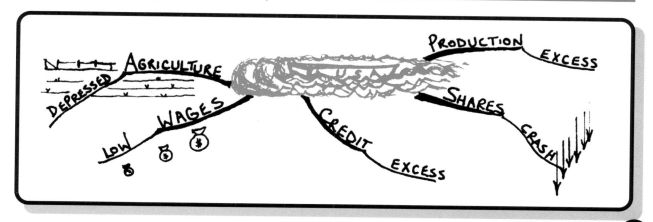

The effects of the Depression

Source A

Economic statistics showing percentage change between 1929 and 1932		
	1929	1932
Share prices	100	17
Overall production	100	60
Wages	100	40
Share dividends	100	43
Foreign trade	100	30
Unemployment	100	600

Source B

'Eleven hundred men standing in a Salvation Army breadline on March 10 1930 near the Bowey Hotel in Manhattan, descended upon two trucks delivering baked goods to the hotel … Cookies, rolls and bread were flung into the street with the hungry jobless chasing after them.'

Irving Bernstein: *The Lean Years* (1960)

Source C

'Eleven children in that house. They've got no shoes, no pants. In the house, no chairs. My God, you go in there, you cry, that's all.'

A Philadelphia shopkeeper reported in *The Nation* (1932)

Source D

'I couldn't go out in the evening to mail a letter without being stopped by nicely dressed men who had told their wives they were out looking for night work. So they were – they were out on the streets cadging dimes and quarters.'

Alistair Cooke, writing of the early 1930s: *America* (1973)

Specimen questions

Study the sources. What evidence do they offer that:

1 by 1932 American trade and industry had seriously declined;

2 the depression had hit most classes of people in the USA;

3 in some places there was real want and a mood of despair;

4 law and order were threatened by the depression?

[15 marks]

Hoover and the Depression

President Hoover (1929–33) did not think the government could do much to end the Depression. He thought the country would have to wait until business recovered of its own accord. But he did a little. The Mind Map will remind you.

Notes

1 The RFC was the Reconstruction Finance Corporation.

2 Increased tariffs were intended to make imports more expensive and so encourage people to buy American goods.

3 Taxes were reduced to encourage people to spend.

Source A

'In Hoover we trusted, now we are busted'

Banner carried by unemployed workers

'Hoovervilles'

Name given to shanty towns built and inhabited by the homeless

Source B

'The Country needs ... and demands bold, persistent experimentation ... Above all, try something.'

F Roosevelt: Campaign speech, 1932

Specimen questions

1 What evidence is there that Hoover's measures were ineffective? [5 marks]

Hint

Use your knowledge as well as the sources.

2 What evidence is there that many people blamed Hoover for the situation? Would he have thought this fair? Explain your answer.

[8 marks]

Hint

To answer this question you need to point out what Hoover did to try to improve the situation, as well as dealing with his views on the helplessness of the government.

3 Why in 1932 would people be more likely to vote for Roosevelt than for Hoover? [3 marks]

check

Make up your own Mind Map showing the effects of the Depression.

The New Deal

Roosevelt's policies

Roosevelt was elected President in November 1932. He took over in March 1933 and set to work at once.

Roosevelt used many ideas to try to solve America's problems. If an idea worked, he persisted with it. If it did not, he dropped it and tried something else. He never gave up.

He tried so many different schemes it is difficult to keep track of them all. The Mind Map on the next page might look detailed, but it gives only a rough idea of all that he did.

Source A

'First of all let me assert my firm belief that the only thing we have to fear is fear itself ... Our greatest primary task is to put people to work ... It can be accomplished in part by direct recruiting by the government itself, treating the task as we would the emergency of a war but at the same time ... accomplishing greatly needed projects.'

President Roosevelt: Inaugural address, 1933

Source B

'In other periods of depression it has always been possible to see some things which were solid and on which you could base hope, but as I look about, I now see nothing to give ground for hope.'

Ex President Coolidge: Speech, 1933

Specimen question

What was the main difference between Coolidge's attitude to the Depression and that of Roosevelt? Explain your answer. [5 marks]

Specimen question

Study the Mind Map. How did the CCC, the TVA, the EHS and the WPA help to 'put people to work' and accomplish 'greatly needed projects'? [10 marks]

Notes

AAA	Agricultural Adjustment Act
CCC	Civilian Conservation Corps
EHS	Emergency Housing Section
FLSA	Fair Labour Standards Act
HOLC	Home Owners Loan Corporation
NRA	National Recovery Administration
SSA	Social Security Act
TVA	Tennessee Valley Authority
WPA	Works Progress Administration

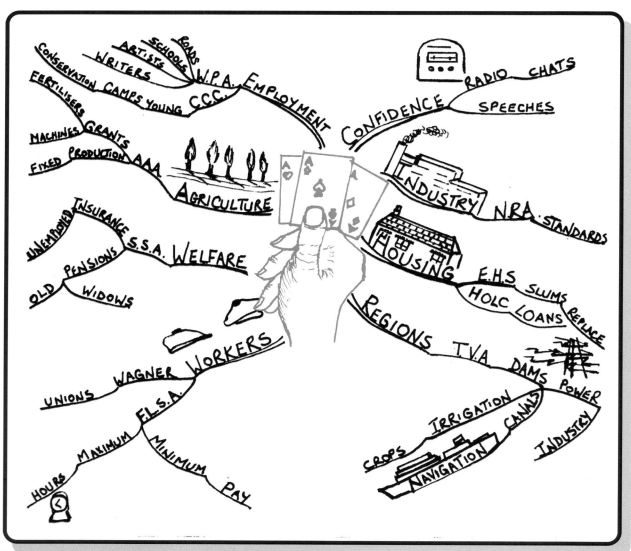

Roosevelt and the people

Source A

A cartoon published in the *New York Daily News* in 1933

Source B

'They missed the way the President used to talk to them. They'd say, "He used to talk to me about my government". There was a real dialogue between Franklin and the people.'

Reaction of people to Roosevelt's death, described by Mrs Roosevelt: *When FDR died* (1961)

Source C

Dear Mr President,

'This is just to tell you everything is all right now. The man you sent found our house all right and we went down to the bank with him and the mortgage can go on for a while longer … I never heard of a President like you, Mr Roosevelt … God bless you.'

Letter sent to President Roosevelt in 1936

Specimen questions

1 What means did President Roosevelt use to keep in touch with the American people?
[2 marks]

2 What evidence is there that he was successful?
[4 marks]

Hint

Look at all three sources.

3 What agency, do you think, had helped the man who wrote Source C? Explain your answer.
[4 marks]

Hint

Study the Mind Map.

4 Study the Mind Map. What schemes did President Roosevelt introduce to improve life for ordinary people?
[6 marks]

5 In April 1936 Time magazine wrote, 'Today, with few exceptions, members of the so-called Upper Class frankly hate Franklin Roosevelt'. Why was this?
[10 marks]

Hints

Roosevelt increased taxes to pay for his reforms. Roosevelt increased the power of the trade unions. Roosevelt tried to control big business. Roosevelt took power into his own hands.

check

that you understand what Roosevelt did to counter the Great Depression.

History Revision Guide

The results of the New Deal

Source A

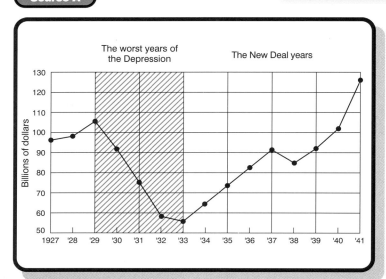

The Gross National Product of the USA 1927–41 (1929 prices)

Source B

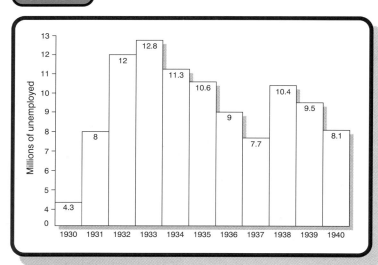

Unemployment in the USA 1930–40

Specimen question

'The New Deal was successful in solving the economic problems of the Depression in the USA.' Do you agree? Explain your answer fully.

[15 marks]

Hints

- As usual in questions like this, the safest answer is one which agrees up to a point.

- Notice that the question asks only about economic problems. So writing a lot about, for instance, social security and housing will get you few, if any, marks.

- Remember that there is no right or wrong answer to this question. The examiners want to see if you can say what you think, and back it up with evidence.

A good way to approach the question would be:

1 To point out that, according to the sources, by 1940
   (a) Gross National Product (GNP) had recovered to near that in 1930;
   (b) unemployment had fallen, but not to the level of 1930.

   So the economic problems seem to have been at least partly solved.

2 To say that, even without the New Deal, the USA economy would probably have picked up in any case.

3 To point out that the quickest recovery in GNP and employment happened after the outbreak of war in 1939 when the USA was increasing production to help in the war against Germany.

4 To conclude that the impact of the New Deal was limited. But it gave people confidence and at least helped the economy to pick up more quickly than it would have otherwise.

check

that you know how far the New Deal was a success.

70

The Ku Klux Klan

The Klan was a racist organisation founded in the Southern states of the USA in 1865 to prevent black Americans being treated as equal to whites. It was revived in 1915, targeting Jews and Roman Catholics as well as blacks. The Mind Map will remind you of its main features.

Notes

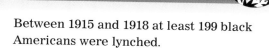

Between 1915 and 1918 at least 199 black Americans were lynched.

Between 1919 and 1922, 239 more were killed.

In 1919 a race riot in Chicago lasted 13 days: 15 whites and 23 blacks were killed.

Specimen question

Why did the Ku Klux Klan grow so quickly between 1915 and 1924, and then decline in numbers so suddenly?   [15 marks]

Model answer

Between 1914 and 1929 American industry boomed, while after 1919 agriculture was less prosperous. Agricultural workers thought they would be better off working in industrial towns than in the countryside. So they moved in. Many were blacks from the Southern states. Some had fought in the war, and thought they deserved equal rights, as was the case in Europe.

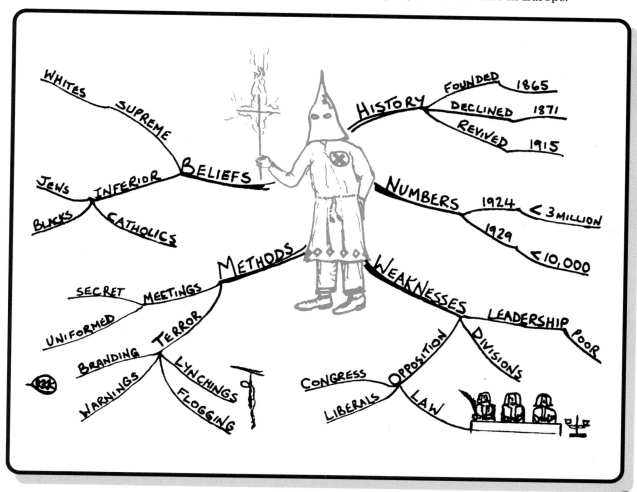

4

This alarmed many traditionalists. They feared that the outsiders would bring in new races, different religions, trade unions and strikes, and so destroy their traditional way of life. So they joined the Klan to keep the newcomers 'in their place' and, if possible, drive them out.

In 1921 Congress investigated the Klan and found it guilty of violence, immorality and corruption. For a time it concentrated on political activity. Many Americans approved of its aims and, as long as it seemed respectable, joined it, so that its membership reached almost 3 million in 1924.

But the Klan's leaders quarrelled among themselves and there were strong rumours of immorality and more stories of violence. So opposition to the Klan increased, while at the same time the country's growing prosperity quietened the fears of many of its supporters. So it lost members, though it was never disbanded.

Blacks were often treated as second-class citizens.

Source A

'No State shall make or enforce any law which shall abridge [reduce] the priveleges or immunities [rights] of citizens of the United States.'

Article 14 of the Constitution of the USA, passed in 1868

Notes

This article was intended to ensure that all citizens of the USA had equal rights. In 1892 Homer Plessey, who was black, complained that his rights were 'abridged' because in Louisiana there were separate railway carriages for white and black passengers. In 1896 the Supreme Court said that, provided the separate facilities were 'equal', they were within the law. This cleared the way, for example, for separate schools, hospitals, barracks and buses.

Source B

'The right of citizens of the United States to vote shall not be denied ... on account of race [or] colour.'

Article 15 of the Constitution of the United States, passed in 1870

Source C

'Mississippi adopted a poll tax and a literacy test as requirements for voters in 1890, and by 1910 every southern state had adopted some [such] type of scheme. These provisions eliminated virtually all Afro-Americans from the voting lists.'

Kenneth C Goode: *From Africa to the United States* (1969)

Specimen questions

1 Explain why Source B did not make the schemes described in Source C illegal.

[4 marks]

2 Using the sources and your own knowledge, explain why many black Americans felt they were denied their rights as US citizens.

[10 marks]

check

that you understand the reasons for the rise and decline of the Klan.

The Second World War

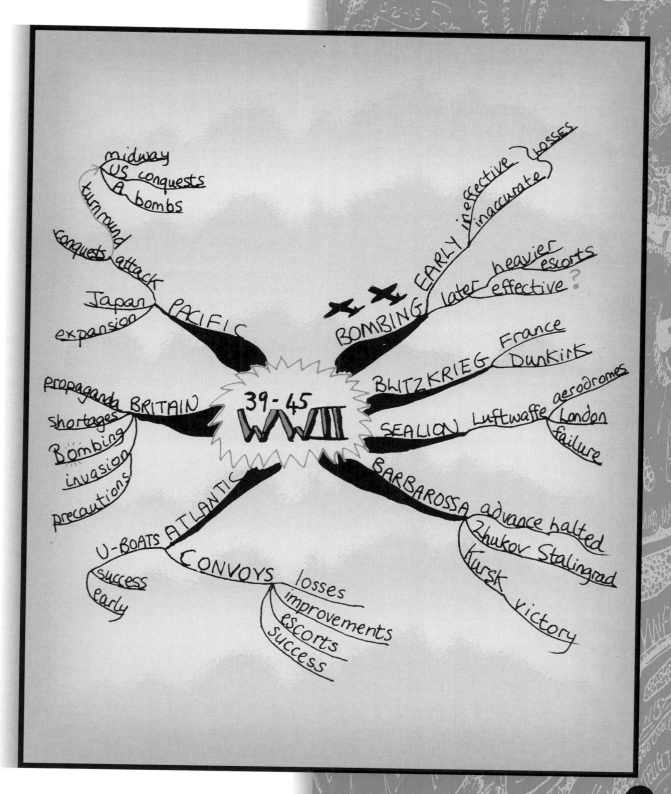

preview
What you need to know

- **How the Germans defeated Allied armies in the early months**

- **How the Luftwaffe tried to win control of the air over England**

- **How Hitler attempted to conquer the USSR**

- **How the German navy tried to get and keep control of the Atlantic**

- **The war between the USA and Japan in the Far East**

- **How the two sides used bombers in the war in Europe**

- **How the Second World War affected life in Britain**

The Blitzkrieg 1939–40

The German generals decided to use a new system of war called Blitzkrieg, in which dive-bombers suddenly attacked enemy roads, railways and airfields while tanks and motorised infantry advanced as fast as they could. By the time the defenders realised what was happening, it was too late.

Notes

The Germans did not attack between the end of September 1939 and April 1940 because they had used up all their supplies of fuel and ammunition in defeating Poland.

The French had not bothered to fortify the Ardennes, where the Germans broke through, because they thought the country was too rough for an invading army to cross.

German attacks in May 1940

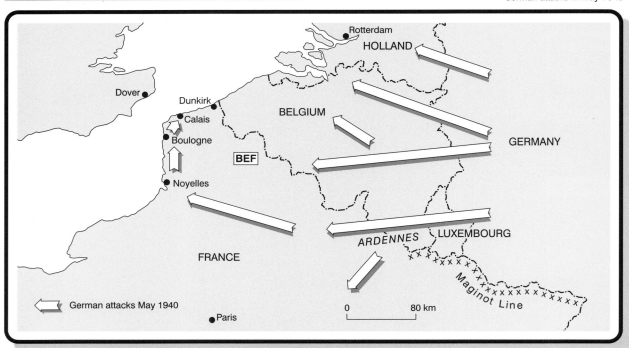

German attacks May 1940

0   80 km

The Blitzkrieg timetable

Sept 1939	German and Soviet troops overran Poland.
April 1940	Germany occupied Denmark and Norway.
May 1940	Germany invaded Holland, Belgium and France.
June 1940	France surrendered.

Source A

'When we have devoted so much effort to building up a fortified barrier [the Maginot Line] do you imagine that we would be mad enough to go out in front of this barrier into all sorts of danger?'

French Minister of War in a speech to the National Assembly

Source B

'The [German] thrust could have been stopped ... by a concentrated counterstroke with similar forces. But the French, though having more and better tanks than the enemy, had strung them out in small packets in the 1918 way.'

B Liddell Hart (British General): *Memoirs* (1965)

Specimen question

Study Sources A and B. Were the French prepared for war in 1940? Explain your answer.

[4 marks]

Hint

Like many questions in history, there is no straightforward 'right' answer.

Model answer

In a way the French were prepared because they had built the Maginot Line and equipped their army with large numbers of modern tanks. On the other hand they were not prepared to fight an attacking war, and did not know how to use tanks effectively. So they had the right equipment and the wrong ideas.

Dunkirk

The British army in France was driven back to the coast. Between 27 May and 3 June 1940, 338,226 men were evacuated from Dunkirk to Britain. Nobody had expected so many to get back. At the time the British press and radio gave the impression that most were rescued by the owners of countless boats and small ships who sailed across to fetch them.

Source A

'All day and all night men of the undefeated British Expeditionary Force have been coming home ... It is clear that if they have not come back in triumph they have come back in glory ... that they **know** they did not meet their masters.'

BBC Radio News, 31 May 1940

Source B

'I was seven years old in 1940 ... When I began to write this book, I struggled to substantiate the familiar belief that an armada of "little ships" played a significant part in the rescue of the army ... I realised that this was false. The little ships operated only on the last two days of the British evacuation, and then to very little effect.'

Nicholas Harman, *Dunkirk: The Necessary Myth* (1980)

Specimen questions

1. Was the radio announcer telling the truth when he said the British Expeditionary Force was 'undefeated'? Explain your answer.　　　　[4 marks]

2. What reasons can you suggest to explain how the popular story of the 'little ships' came into being?　　　　[4 marks]

3. Do you believe what Nicholas Harman says about the evacuation? Explain your answer.　　　　[4 marks]

4. 'The successes of the German army in 1940 were due to Allied mistakes.' Do you agree? Explain your answer fully.　　　　[15 marks]

Hints

You can use your own knowledge as well as the sources to answer this. The safest way to tackle questions like this is to strike a balance. So, the Allies did make mistakes. For example:

1 Displaying a general lack of confidence and initiative.

2 Not attacking the Germans while they were still re-stocking after invading Poland.

3 Not fortifying the Ardennes.

4 Not using their tanks effectively.

But, the Germans fought well. For example:

1 Their troops were full of confidence.

2 Their Blitzkrieg tactics – explain them – were new and effective.

3 Their sudden, unprovoked attacks – give examples – gave opponents no time to organise or fight back.

Come to a conclusion.

Norway

The German attack on Norway brought about a change in the British government. Norway was important because Sweden exported iron ore to Germany through the Norwegian port of Narvik. In addition, Norway was the shortest route to get help to Finland, which was fighting against the USSR.

Norway timetable

5 February	British government approved an attack on Narvik.
13 March	Finland surrendered to the USSR.
14 March	Attack on Narvik cancelled.
26 March	Plan to attack Narvik approved again.
2 April	Chamberlain made a speech, claiming *'Hitler has missed the bus'*.
9 April	German troops overran Denmark and invaded Norway.
14–17 April	British troops landed at Namsos, Narvik and Andalsnes.
29 April	British troops landed at Bodo.
2 & 3 May	British troops evacuated from Namsos and Andalsnes.
7 & 8 May	Debate in House of Commons which forced Chamberlain to resign.

Specimen question

Study the timetable. What evidence is there in it of the British government's

(a) complacency

(b) indecision and bad planning?　　　　[5 marks]

that you understand how the Germans won so many victories in 1939 and 1940.

The Battle of Britain

After the fall of France, Hitler decided to invade England (Operation Sealion). He needed the Luftwaffe to escort the invasion barges full of troops across the Channel. First he had to destroy the RAF.

Between 12 August and 7 September 1940 German bombers and fighters attacked British air bases. In this time they destroyed about 630 fighters. But they believed they had destroyed more than 3,000. So Göring, head of the Luftwaffe, thought he had defeated the RAF and decided to attack London instead.

The biggest raid was on 15 September. RAF fighters shot down 60 German planes. The RAF lost 26. Göring realised that the RAF was too strong for Germany to risk invading England. Hitler cancelled his invasion plans.The Mind Map shows why the RAF won the Battle of Britain.

Notes

★ **Range**

Fighters did not carry enough fuel to fly long distances. So the RAF had an advantage flying close to their bases.

★ **Radar**

Radar showed exactly where the German planes were. So the RAF did not have to waste time and fuel looking for them.

★ **Pilots**

Pilots whose planes were shot down in the battle often parachuted down over southern England or into the sea nearby. German pilots were picked up and imprisoned. British pilots were available to go on flying. So the RAF needed fewer replacements than the Luftwaffe.

★ **Planes**

Lord Beaverbrook was in charge of aircraft production. Britain's factories produced more planes than the Luftwaffe destroyed during the Battle of Britain. Germany's aircraft factories were badly organised.

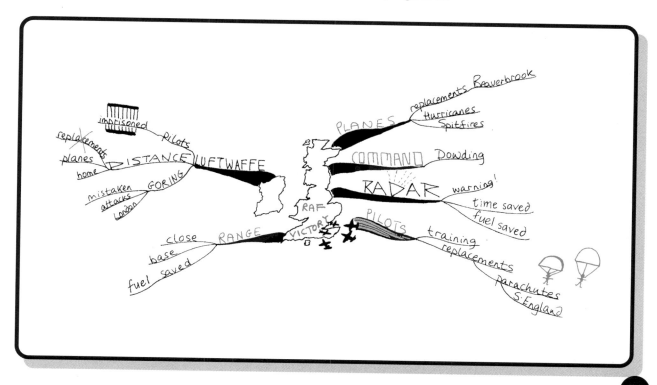

5

Source A

'This switch to London from military targets, from air bases, changed the situation for Great Britain and Fighter Command considerably. If we would have continued to attack the bases perhaps the situation would have been changed.'

Adolf Galland, 1940 Luftwaffe Wing Commander: Television interview, 1973

Source B

'The attack didn't go to the airfields. It went to London. And the airfields were spared so they were able to pull themselves together, sort themselves out, repair things and, most important of the lot, give the pilots more of a chance for a little rest.'

Robert Wright, a member of Dowding's staff in 1940: Television interview, 1973

Specimen question

Read Sources A and B. Which of the two speakers was likely to know more about the situation in the Battle of Britain? Explain your answer. [4 marks]

Hints

Galland flew in the war in the air. What would he have known about conditions on the ground? Wright was on Dowding's staff. Would he have had more complete information? Extra credit for spotting that by 1973 they might both have done research and so know about the same information.

Specimen question

Are Sources A and B strong evidence that the RAF would have been defeated if the Luftwaffe had continued to attack the airfields? Explain your answer. [10 marks]

Hints

Remember that you can use your own knowledge of the topic as well as the sources to answer the question, and that the examiner is more interested in the way you use the evidence than in the conclusion you reach.

Does either source suggest that continuing to attack the airfields would certainly have defeated the RAF? Does either offer strong evidence that the situation was serious? Give examples.

What continuing advantages did the RAF possess? Come to a conclusion.

check

that you understand why the RAF won the Battle of Britain.

Barbarossa – Invasion of the Soviet Union

In June 1941, without any warning, German troops invaded the Soviet Union. The Mind Map will remind you of Hitler's motives.

Hitler thought it would be easy. *'We have only to kick in the door and the whole rotten structure will come crashing down'*, he told General Jodl. The map shows you how far the German army penetrated into the Soviet Union.

Maps can help you to understand and remember. Try drawing you own to help with revision.

Problems for Germany

Early in the campaign there were warning signs that the invasion was not going Hitler's way.

Source A

'When the war began we had expected 200 enemy divisions. Now we have already counted 350. These divisions are certainly not properly armed and equipped as we would see it and they are often lacking in tactical leadership. But they are there. And whenever a dozen of these divisions are destroyed, the Russians replace them with another dozen.'

Franz Halder, German army Chief of Staff: *Diary*, 11 August 1941

Source B

'We had no gloves. We had no winter shoes. We had no equipment whatsoever to fight or withstand the cold ... Due to the cold we lost a lot of people who got frost-bitten ... As it became colder ... most of our artillery had become completely unusable. Guns didn't fire any more.'

Ekkehard Maurer, German army officer: Television interview, 1973

Source C

'We saw [Siberian troops] after taking this small village ... Very big men with very good winter clothes ... And then my feeling was a very bad one, because this was the sign that the Russian people, the Russian government was able to take troops from the far east and to transport them to the front at Moscow.'

Rolf Elble, German army officer: Television interview, 1973

Specimen question

Study the sources. In what ways do they show that the Germans had underestimated the difficulties of fighting against the Soviet Union?   [8 marks]

Soviet recovery

After 1941 the Soviet Union recovered. It set up vast new factories in the east and recruited new armies. So production increased as did the size of the army.

The Soviet planners used their resources sensibly. They chose a few robust, reliable weapons and built huge numbers of them. Also Stalin, their leader, learned by his mistakes. He had taken all the important military decisions in the first year of the war. He was not a professional soldier and he had often been wrong. After 1942 he usually followed the advice of Marshal Georgi Zhukov, the Deputy Commissar of Defence, who understood modern warfare. Under his command, the Soviet army began to win battles.

Make your own Mind Map showing why the Soviet Union began to win battles after 1942.

Stalingrad timetable

July 1942	Hitler ordered a three-fold attack, on the Caucasus, Leningrad and Stalingrad.
Sept 1942	German troops entered the outskirts of Stalingrad.
8 Nov 1942	Hitler boasted: 'We've got it ... No-one will ever be able to get us out now'.
23 Nov 1942	Soviet armies surrounded German forces in Stalingrad.
31 Jan 1943	German commander, Von Paulus, surrendered with 90,000 men.

Source A

'The Germans could not stand close fighting ... They could not bear us to come close to them when we counter-attacked ... We should get as close to the enemy as possible ... Every German soldier must be made to feel he was living under the muzzle of a Russian gun.'

General Chuikov, Soviet commander of Stalingrad: *The Beginning of the Road* (1963)

Source B

'Stalingrad is Hell on earth ... We attack every day. If we capture twenty yards in the morning the Russians throw us back again in the evening.'

Letter from a German NCO serving in Stalingrad

Specimen question

Historians agree that General Chuikov was the right man to send to command the Soviet forces in Stalingrad. Do the sources support this view? Explain your answer.
[4 marks]

Model answer

Yes, the sources do support this view because he found out that the Germans did not like hand-to-hand fighting. To exploit this he told his troops to keep as close to the Germans as possible. This proved very successful, helping to create 'a Hell on earth' for the Germans.

Specimen question

Why was Stalingrad a 'Hell on earth' for the German troops?
[8 marks]

Hints

Your are *not* tied to the sources in this question. You can use your own knowledge of the topic as well. There is not one, full, correct answer. The examiners will be looking for perhaps six relevant points, backed up with examples.

You might mention: cold, hunger, lack of supplies, fear of the enemy, poor medical facilities, distance from home, unfamiliar battle tactics (e.g. remember they were trained for Blitzkrieg, not house-to-house fighting), desolation of their surroundings, gradually increasing sense of hopelessness.

Hitler's leadership

Source A

'[Hitler] had his own picture of the world and every fact had to be fitted into that personal picture ... But in fact it was a picture of another world.'

General Guderian, (Hitler's Chief of Staff 1944–5): *Panzer Leader* (1952)

Source B

'When a statement was read to him which showed that Stalin would be able to muster another ... million men north of Stalingrad ... Hitler flew at the man who was reading with clenched fists and foam in the corners of his mouth and forbade him to read such idiotic twaddle.'

Franz Halder (Hitler's Chief of Staff 1938–42): *Hitler as Warlord* (1950)

Source C

'Our enemies rightly regarded this disaster at Stalingrad as a turning point in the war. But at Hitler's headquarters the only reaction was a temporary numbness.'

Albert Speer (Hitler's armaments minister): *Inside the Third Reich* (1970)

Specimen questions

1. Study the sources. Do Sources B and C confirm Guderian's view of how Hitler's mind worked? Explain your answer. [5 marks]

2. Do you think the information contained in these sources reliable? Explain your answer. [4 marks]

Hints

Were the authors in a position to know? Do they tell the same story? Had they any motive for lying?

Soviet victory

Source A

A cartoon published in the Soviet Union in 1942

Specimen questions

1 Was the cartoon an accurate representation of the situation in 1942? Explain your answer.
[5 marks]

Hints

Strength of Hitler? Part played by the USA and Britain in 1942?

2 Why, do you think, did the Soviet government publish the cartoon in 1942? [3 marks]

Source B

The Soviet advance

In July 1943 there was a huge battle at Kursk, where the Germans lost 2,700 tanks and 900,000 men. They were now much weaker than the Soviets (*see* the table).

German and Soviet military strength 1943		
	Men	**Tanks**
German	2.5 million	2,300
Soviets	5.5 million	8,400

The Soviet army advanced steadily (*see* map). The Russian war ended in May 1945 when Soviet troops captured Berlin. The Soviet Union had defeated Hitler, but in so doing had lost 20 million people.

People in Britain and the USA have often not given enough credit to the part played by the Soviet Union in the defeat of Germany. They have concentrated instead on the campaigns fought by British and American troops in North Africa and Italy, and on the invasion of Northern France in 1944. But in 1945 only 35 German divisions were fighting against British and American troops. More than 200 were fighting the Soviet army in the east.

Specimen question

Why was the part played by the Soviet Union in the war neglected by people in Britain and the USA? [5 marks]

Hints

Cold War? Patriotism?

check

that you understand how and why the Soviet Union defeated the Germans.

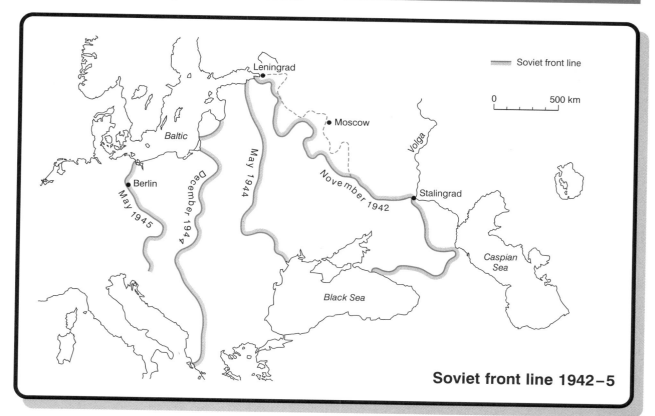

Soviet front line 1942–5

Soviet front line

0 — 500 km

Leningrad
Moscow
Baltic
Berlin
May 1944
December 1944
May 1945
Volga
November 1942
Stalingrad
Caspian Sea
Black Sea

The Battle of the Atlantic

The most important sea battle of the war was fought by German U-boats trying to prevent supplies crossing the Atlantic to Britain. Merchant ships were grouped together into convoys escorted by warships and aircraft. The U-boats attacked them in the 'Mid-Atlantic Gap' while they were out of range of aircraft based on land.

In 1942, U-boats sank 5.4 million tons of Allied shipping, and reduced Britain's imports to a third of what they had been in 1939. But during 1943 the number of U-boats destroyed increased (*see* table). You need to know why this happened. The Mind Map will remind you.

U-boats destroyed	
Mar 1943	15
Apr 1943	19
May 1943	41

Notes

★ **Intelligence**
The Admiralty was able to tell the convoys where the U-boats were likely to be.

★ **Training**
The navy and air force improved the training of the crew of ships and planes escorting the convoys.

★ **Technology**
VLR (Very Long Range) aircraft could 'cover' more of the ocean.
Planes carried Leigh lights which could light up U-boats on the surface at night.
New Centrimetric radar enabled aircraft to spot U-boats on the surface more easily.

★ **Portugal**
In October 1943 Portugal allowed the Allies to use an air base on the Azores. This closed the Mid-Atlantic gap.

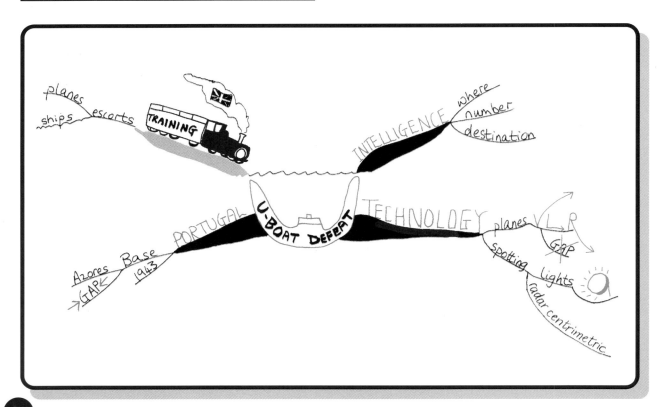

Source A

'The submarine will in the end decide the outcome of the war.'

Hitler, June 1942

Source B

'The only peril that ever frightened me during the war was the U-boat peril'

Winston Churchill: *The Second World War* (1950)

Source C

'Enemy aircraft have been equipped with a new location apparatus ... which enables them to detect submarines and to attack them unexpectedly in low cloud, bad visibility or at night ... Losses have risen from 14 submarines, that is about 13% of those at sea, to 36 submarines, or perhaps 37, that is about 30% of the submarines at sea. These losses are too high.'

Admiral Dönitz: Memorandum to Hitler, May 1943.

Specimen questions

1. In May 1943 Dönitz withdrew the U-boats from the North Atlantic. What would **(a)** Hitler and **(b)** Churchill have thought of this? Explain your answer. [4 marks]

2. Dönitz mentions only one reason for growing U-boat losses. Why, do you think, did he not mention the others shown on the Mind Map? [4 marks]

3. Why was Dönitz careful to quote exact numbers in his memorandum? [4 marks]

Hint

Look at Source A. Would it be easy to persuade Hitler to withdraw the U-boats?

Merchant seamen

Source

'More than 32,000 died at sea during World War II, all of them volunteers, out of a total of about 145,000. The overall casualty rate in the British Merchant Navy during World War II was higher than that in any of the armed services ... British Merchant seamen were never actually compelled to sign on for another voyage ... These civilians went back to sea again time after time simply because they were sailors and thought they should.'

Mark Arnold-Forster: *The World at War* (1973)

Specimen questions

1. How does the writer try to make the reader share his admiration for merchant seamen? [3 marks]

2. Does the fact that the writer admires merchant seamen make the figures he quotes unreliable? Explain your answer. [4 marks]

check

that you understand how important the war in the Atlantic was, and how the Allies won it.

The Pacific war

Outbreak

After 1900 Japan's industry developed rapidly, but she needed raw materials and overseas markets to sell what she produced. She needed an empire, but most of the territories in the area belonged to other countries. The Japanese realised that they might have to fight for what they wanted, and built up their armed forces.

Specimen questions

1 How could the USA have justified their refusal to sell oil to Japan? [2 marks]

2 How could Japan have justified their attack on Pearl Harbor? [2 marks]

> Remember, tables are a compact way of presenting information. Try compiling your own to help with your revision.

Japanese expansion timetable

1910	Japan annexed Korea.
1914	Japan took over Germany's Pacific colonies.
1931	Japan invaded Manchuria.
1933	Japan left the League of Nations.
1941 **July:**	Japan occupied French Indo-China. USA banned oil exports to Japan (90 per cent of Japan's oil).
Dec:	Japan attacked Pearl Harbor. Sank 14 US warships. Destroyed more than 300 aircraft. 3,500 US casualties. USA and Britain declared war on Japan. Germany declared war on the USA.

Japanese victories

After Pearl Harbor, Japanese armies quickly overran much of the Pacific. The Mind Map will remind you how the Japanese were able to take over so much land so quickly.

Japanese victories timetable

Dec 1941	Invaded Malaya, captured Guam, Wake, Hong Kong.
Feb 1942	Captured Singapore.
Mar 1942	Conquered the Dutch East Indies.
April 1942	Conquered Burma.
May 1942	Conquered the Philippines.

Furthest extent of Japanese occupation July 1942

Areas occupied by Japanese on surrender 25 August 1945

In July 1942 Japan controlled large oil reserves
70% of world's tin
90% of world's rubber

The USA counter-attack

In the Pacific war, control of the sea was vital to protect the ships carrying troops and supplies to the islands. The most important warships were aircraft carriers, whose planes could bomb and sink enemy battleships. When the Japanese attacked Pearl Harbor the US navy's four largest aircraft carriers were out at sea and so were safe.

In June 1942 the Japanese decided to capture Midway Island. The US navy broke Japanese codes and were waiting for them. In 10 minutes US planes sank 4 Japanese aircraft carriers and killed or injured 240 of Japan's best pilots.

> **Source**
>
> *'After Midway I was certain there was no chance of success.'*
>
> Mitsumasa Yonai (Japanese Navy Minister, when interrogated after the war)

Specimen question

Why, do you think, did the Battle of Midway convince Mitsumasa Yonai that Japan could not win the war?   [3 marks]

The A bombs

The USA began to recapture the islands taken by Japan. And when they were close enough they began to bomb Japan itself. In August 1945 they dropped two atom bombs, one on Hiroshima and one on Nagasaki. Japan surrendered.

Source A

'The Japanese were tough fighters. They never would give up ... We tried to persuade the Japanese to surrender. But they kept fighting ... and we soldiers had to annihilate them. They would not surrender.'

US General Collins describing an attack on Guadacanal: Television interview, 1973

Source B

'Between April and August 1945 21st Bomber Command ... destroyed 40 percent of the built up area of 66 cities ... A combination of sea blockade and bombing reduced most Japanese industries to a mere fraction of their wartime peak. By July aluminium production was reduced to 9 percent, oil refining and steel production to 15 percent.'

Richard Overy: *Why the Allies Won* (1995)

Source C

'We said that we didn't think that being scientists especially qualified us as to how to answer this question of how the [A] bombs should be used or not ... We did say that we did not think that exploding one of these things as a firecracker over a desert was likely to be very impressive.'

Scientific panel advising US government in 1945

Source D

'The final decision of where and when to use the atomic bomb was up to me. Let there be no mistake about it. I regarded the bomb as a military weapon and never had any doubts that it should be used.'

US President Harry S Truman: *Memoirs* (1955)

Source E

'The decision to use the atomic bomb ... brought death to over a hundred thousand Japanese ... but this deliberate, premeditated destruction of Hiroshima and Nagasaki put an end to the Japanese war. It stopped the fire raids and the strangling blockade; it ended the ghastly spectre of a clash of great armies.'

Henry Stimson, US Secretary of War in 1945

Specimen questions

1 Read Source D.
   (a) In what ways did the A bomb differ from other military weapons? [2 marks]

   (b) Why, do you think, did Harry Truman describe his decision to drop the bomb in such a matter-of-fact way?

   [3 marks]

Hints

Was the decision to drop the bomb controversial? Would Truman like controversy? How might he stop people criticising him?

2 Read Sources A and C.
   How do these sources support dropping the bomb? [4 marks]

3 Read Source B.
   Do the facts quoted in this source argue against dropping the bomb? Explain your answer. [6 marks]

Hint

Remember there may be no right answer to this. Whatever you think, you must give good reasons for your view. That is what the examiner is interested in.

Model answer

Overy (Source B) shows that conventional bombing and the blockade were destroying Japanese towns and had badly damaged the country's industry. This meant that even without the A bomb she would probably have lost the war. But this doesn't disprove the case that the A bombs saved lives by ending the war quickly. This was the main argument in favour of using the bomb. So it doesn't necessarily argue against dropping the bomb. In any case, President Truman could not have known at the time how weak Japanese industry was.

Specimen question

Read Source E.
Was Henry Stimson in favour of dropping the bomb? Explain your answer.   [4 marks]

check

that you understand how and why Japan was defeated.

The Mind Map sums up the reasons why Japan lost the war.

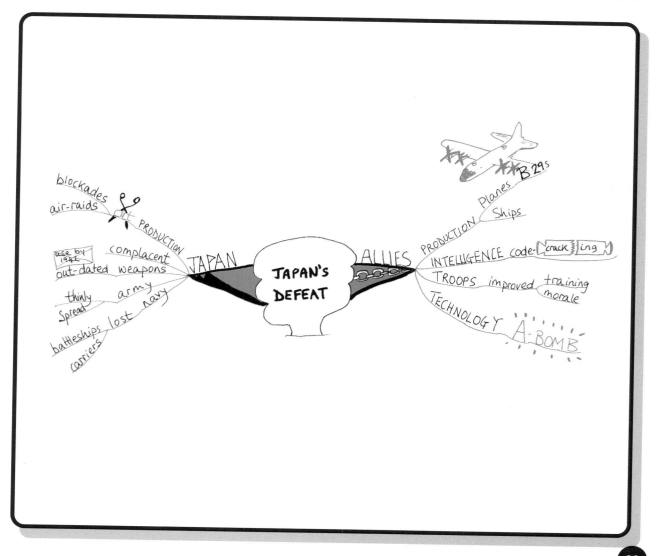

5

The bombing war

People still argue about the bombing war. Some say it was a waste of men, material and money. Others say it helped to shorten the war in Europe. You need to know how effective you think it was and to be able to back up your opinion with evidence.

British raids on Germany 1940–2

After the defeat of France, British bombers attacked German factories and railways. It was the only way Britain could attack Germany.

Heavy "Stirling" bombers raid the Nazi Baltic port of Lübeck and leave the docks ablaze

BACK THEM UP!

This poster shows British bombers attacking Lübeck

Source B

In 1941, after examining aerial photographs, a civil servant, D M Butt, worked out that only one in five of British bombers managed to get within nine miles of their target. In 1941, 1,034 British bombers were shot down.

Specimen questions

1 Would British civilians who had seen Source A have been surprised by the information in Source B? Explain your answer.   [4 marks]

Hint

Would they believe the poster?

2 Does Source B give the impression that the raids on Germany between 1940 and 1942 were effective?   [2 marks]

German raids on Britain 1940–2

Between 25 August and 4 September 1940 the British bombed Berlin five times. In revenge Hitler ordered the Luftwaffe to bomb British cities. Between September 1940 and March 1941 there were regular raids on British cities, killing 21,000 people.

Source A

'We shall obliterate their cities.'
Hitler: Speech, 4 September 1940

Source B

'Last Thursday 180 persons were killed in London as a result of 251 tons of bombs. That is to say it took one ton of bombs to kill three-quarters of a person ... It would take ten years, at the present rate of bombing for half the houses of London to be demolished. [But] quite a lot of things are going to happen to Herr Hitler and the Nazi regime before ten years are up.'

Winston Churchill: House of Commons speech, 8 October 1940

Source C

'You must try to picture the bombed-out as I saw them. White-faced, their homes and lives shattered ... They had crept out of the shelter ... They came past houses with no windows and no roofs, houses split and frontless ... maybe with the furniture showing on each floor ... And as a background to it all, the sirens wailing every few hours, and the drone of bombers overhead, and the whine and crash of bombs, and the everlasting sour smell of smoke.'

Frank R Lewey, Mayor of Stepney: Interview

Specimen questions

1 Was Hitler's threat to 'obliterate' Britain's cities realistic? Explain your answer.

[4 marks]

2 Is Churchill's calculation in Source B to be trusted? Explain your answer. [4 marks]

Hints

How did Churchill know the exact tonnage of bombs dropped on London on a particular night? What were the aims of his speech in the House of Commons? How might they have biased what he said?

3 Source C describes what it was like to be bombed out of one's home. Yet Hitler's Blitz did not destroy civilian morale in Britain? Why was this? [6 marks]

Bombing Germany 1942–4

In 1942 Churchill met Stalin and promised to help the Soviet Union by bombing Germany. By this time 'Bomber' Harris was in charge of Bomber Command. He believed that bombing large towns would eventually destroy the morale of the people living there and disrupt their working lives, thus cutting production and hindering the war effort.

> **Facts and figures**
>
> **Night raids**
>
> In March 1944, 1,719 bombers were sent to Berlin. Only 27 dropped their bombs within 3 miles of the target.
>
> Up to 10 per cent of the bombers were lost on every raid.
>
> **Daylight raids**
>
> In summer 1943 the US air force began daylight raids. These were more accurate.
>
> More than 20 per cent of the bombers were lost on every raid.
>
> **German war production (000s)**
>
> | | Planes | Tanks |
> |---|---|---|
> | 1941 | 12 | 5 |
> | 1942 | 15 | 9 |
> | 1943 | 25 | 17 |
> | 1944 | 40 | 22 |

Specimen question

Do the facts and figures prove that the Allied bombing of Germany at that time was ineffective? Explain your answer. [5 marks]

Hint

Statistics are tricky. Who is likely to have compiled the figures of German war production? Might they have falsified the figures? What about other commodities? And might the production of tanks and planes have been even higher without the bombing?

Bombing Germany 1944–5

By the end of 1943 the Allies had more heavy bombers and a new long-range fighter – the Mustang. For the first time fighters could escort bombers all the way to Germany and back. They also had more accurate equipment to guide them to their targets. As a result the war in the air over Germany changed.

Source A

'The standard of the Americans is extraordinarily high. Our day fighters have lost more than 1,000 aircraft during the last few months, including our best officers. The gaps cannot be filled.'

Adolf Gallard, German Luftwaffe General: *The First and the Last* (1955)

'There are about 1,000 heavy bombers flying eastwards … with a strong fighter escort … Against them we are forty aircraft.'

H Knoke, a German fighter pilot: 1944 diary

Source B

Tons of bombs dropped on Germany	
1939–44	240,000
1944–5	1,180,000

Source C

'One can't get used to the raids. I wished for an end. We all got nerves. We did not get enough sleep and were very tense. People fainted when they heard the first bomb drop.'

Worker at a Munich factory, 1945

Source D

'The war is over in the area of heavy industry and armament.'

Albert Speer, Minister in charge of War Production: Report to Hitler, January 1945

Source E

'American air intelligence exaggerated German air strength in 1940 by a factor of ten … A new generation of bombers, fighters and fighter bombers … were produced in greater numbers than were needed … to match what it was believed Germany was producing.'

Richard Overy: *Why the Allies Won* (1995)

Specimen questions

1 What evidence is there that by 1945 Bomber Harris had been proved right? [4 marks]

2 What developments made it possible for Allied bombers to destroy German industry by 1945? [4 marks]

3 What evidence is there that the Allied success in the air war was based on a mistake? Explain your answer. [4 marks]

check

that you can explain how the bombing war changed between 1939 and 1945 and how important it was.

The Home Front

The Second World War affected life in Britain in many ways (*see* Mind Map). In some ways – shortages, conscription, rationing – the effects were much the same as in the First World War. But other effects were different:

Bombing

The government expected Britain to be bombed and gassed in the Second World War. So they had prepared for it by building shelters, distributing gas masks, enforcing a blackout, evacuating children from London and other large cities and enlisting voluntary 'wardens' to organise air raid precautions such as watching out for fires caused by incendiary bombs.

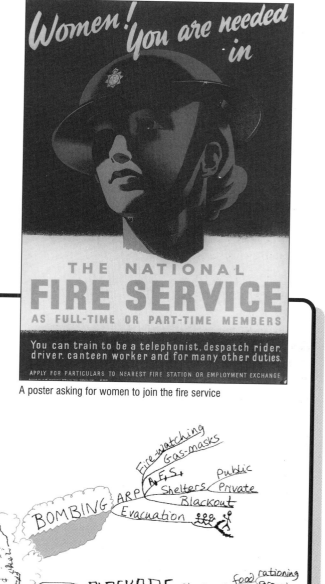

Source

A poster asking for women to join the fire service

(Mind Map — Home Front)

- **INVASION?** — Homeguard, Defences, ~~Signs~~
- **BOMBING** — ARP: Fire-watching, Gas-masks, A.F.S., Shelters (Public, Private), Blackout, Evacuation
- **BRITISH PROPAGANDA** — Posters, papers, BBC, Churchill
- **GERMAN** — radio
- **BLOCKADE** — Shortages: food (rationing, growing), petrol cars, goods
- **MAN POWER** — conscription (men, women)

HOME FRONT

Specimen questions

1. What job, usually performed by firemen, is not mentioned in the list of duties to be performed by women members of the fire service? Why was this, do you think? [3 marks]

2. Compare this poster with the WRAF recruiting poster in Chapter 1. Is there any evidence that the official attitude to what women could do had changed since 1917? Explain your answer. [4 marks]

Invasion

In the First World War Britain was never likely to be invaded. In 1940 it seemed very likely, so the government took precautions, building defences, taking down road signs, and setting up the volunteer Home Guard.

warning!

Dad's Army is a comedy programme, not a documentary.

Propaganda

Propaganda was very important. The coming of radio made it possible to broadcast messages very widely, very quickly. Churchill used it a lot, but both sides broadcast propaganda to their enemies. Both sides also used films, posters and newspapers to get their message across.

Source A

'We shall go on to the end. We shall fight in France, we shall fight on the seas and oceans, we shall fight with growing confidence and growing strength in the air, we shall defend our island, whatever the cost may be. We shall fight on the beaches, we shall fight on the landing grounds, we shall fight in the fields and in the streets, we shall fight in the hills; we shall never surrender.'

Winston Churchill: House of Commons speech, 4 June 1940

Source B

'That was worth 1,000 guns, and the speeches of 1,000 years.'

Josiah Wedgwood, Labour MP, after hearing Churchill's speech

Source C

'The Nation had the lion's heart. I had the luck to give the roar.'

Winston Churchill: Speech, 1954

Specimen questions

1. What effect did Churchill hope his 1940 speech would have on
   (a) the British people
   (b) the Germans? [4 marks]

2. What evidence is there that the speech was successful? [3 marks]

Hint

Use your knowledge as well as the sources.

3. Do you think that Churchill's estimate of his importance in the war was correct? Explain your answer. [10 marks]

Hint

Did he help to give the nation its heart as well as supply the roar? What about his actions and policies?

check

that you understand the effects that the war had on Britain.

Summing up

The Mind Map helps to explain why Germany lost the war.

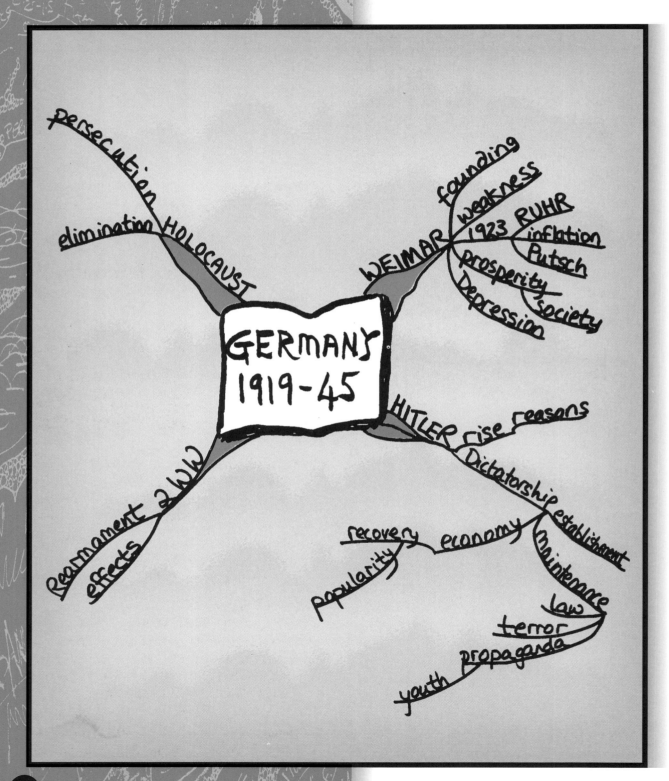

preview
What you need to know

- **How the republican government ruled Germany from 1919 to 1932**
- **How Hitler was voted into office**
- **How Hitler gained complete control of Germany**
- **How the German economy improved between 1933 and 1939**
- **Everyday life in Germany under Hitler**
- **How Hitler dealt with opposition**
- **The effect that the Second World War had on Germany**
- **The Nazi attempt to exterminate the Jews in Europe**

Source A

'I make no bones of the fact that I am a monarchist. My God! when a man has served his king and country faithfully for 30 years he can't suddenly say, "Starting tomorrow I'm a republican." '

Colonel William Reinhard, quoted in O Schuddekopf: *Das Heer und die Republik* (1955)

Source B

'A dazzling lieutenant is of greater importance than the mayor of a great city. The latter may walk through the streets unrecognised, but every policeman, tram-conductor, post or railway official salutes an officer.'

Richard Hanser: *Prelude to Terror* (1971)

Source C

'May the hand wither that signs this treaty'

Philip Scheidemann, German Chancellor: Speech, June 1919

Specimen questions

Study the sources.

1. How far do Sources A and B help to explain why many Germans never had any respect for the Weimar government? [4 marks]

2. Check on the terms of the Versailles Treaty (Chapter 2). Explain why Chancellor Scheidemann was so opposed to signing it. [10 marks]

The Weimar Republic

Foundation

In November 1918 there was a revolution in Germany. The Kaiser's government, dominated by the army, was swept away and replaced at a conference which met at Weimar by a democratically elected government. Most of the new ministers were lawyers and businessmen. The President, Friedrich Ebert, for instance, had worked as a saddler and journalist. The *Reichstag* (Parliament) contained a number of small parties, so that no one party ever had a majority of seats. So governments tended to be weak and divided. Almost their first job was to sign the peace treaty (*see* Chapter 2).

1923 – a critical year

1923 was an important year for the Weimar Republic. The French and Belgians occupied the Ruhr (*see* Chapter 2). The mark lost all its value (*see* Chapter 2) Finally, in the Munich *Putsch* Adolf Hitler tried to take over the government.

In September 1923 the Bavarian state government declared a state of emergency. Some thought they intended to make Bavaria independent of the rest of Germany. The timetable will remind you of what happened next.

Munich Putsch timetable

8 November	Adolf Hitler took over a political meeting in Munich and captured Bavarian government leaders.
9 November	Hitler's march through Munich was dispersed by armed police.
February 1924	Hitler found guilty of treason. Sentenced to five years imprisonment.
December	Hitler released from prison, having written part one of *Mein Kampf*.

Specimen question

Did the events of 1923 weaken or strengthen the Weimar government? Explain your answer.

[10 marks]

Hints

The examiners expect you to come to a conclusion and back it up with evidence and argument. The better your argument, the better your marks.

The safest line is probably to say that in some ways it was weaker, and in other ways stronger. For example, the currency was sorted out by the end of the year, which meant people could get back to work, which strengthened the government, but on the other hand people who had lost all their money in the inflation would blame the government, which weakened it.

Similarly, in the short term, the government defeated and imprisoned Hitler which strengthened it, but his trial gave him publicity and made him a national figure which in the long term helped him to destroy the government.

The prosperous years 1925–9

Between 1925 and 1929 Germany prospered on money borrowed from the USA. The country became famous for its artists and architects. Berlin also became famous for its night life.

Source

A cartoon entitled 'Lovers' little hour' by George Grasz, a left-wing cartoonist. The cartoon shows a rich businessman entertaining a prostitute.

Specimen questions

1 What impression does the source give of German society at the time?   [3 marks]

2 Would the impression strengthen or weaken support for the Weimar government? Explain your answer.   [5 marks]

The Crash

In 1929, after the Wall Street Crash, Americans wanted Germany to repay the money she had borrowed. Suddenly there was no money to spare in Germany. People bought fewer goods. Factories closed and unemployment rose.

German unemployment	
1928	650,000
1929	1,320,000
1930	3,000,000
1931	4,350,000
1932	6,000,000

Specimen question

Why, by 1932, did many Germans want to be rid of the Weimar government? [15 marks]

Hint

The following Mind Map will help you to organise your answer.

check

that you understand why the Weimar government was weak and unpopular.

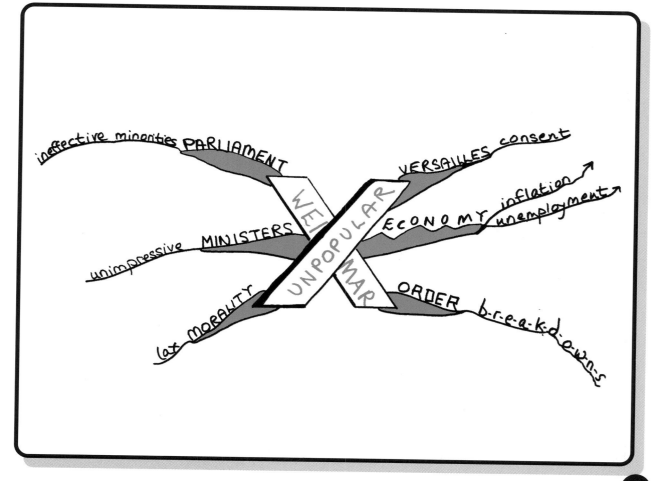

The rise of Hitler

Hitler and the Nazi Party were ready to sweep away the whole Weimar system. The Mind Map will remind you of their beliefs and the way they worked.

The high point of many party meetings and rallies was a speech by Hitler himself.

Source A

'One must be able to say once again: German people, hold your heads high and proudly once more! You are no longer enslaved and in bondage, but you are free again and can truly say: "We are all proud that through God's powerful aid we have once more become true Germans."'

Hitler: Extract from a speech made in March 1933

Source B

'I was held under a hypnotic spell by the sheer force of his conviction. The intense will of the man, the passion of his sincerity, seemed to flow from him into me. It was like a religious conversion.'

A listener to one of Hitler's speeches in 1922

Hitler's rise timetable

1920–3	Hitler organised the Nazi Party.
1923	German inflation – the Munich Putsch.
1924	Hitler imprisoned – wrote *Mein Kampf*.
1925–9	Germany prosperous – Nazis won little support.
1929	Wall Street Crash.
1930	German unemployment reached 15 per cent. Nazis won 107 Reichstag seats.
1932	Unemployment 30 per cent. Nazis won 230 seats (July); 197 (November).
1933	Hitler became Chancellor (Prime Minister).

Notice how much information can be crammed into a table. Compile your own to help with your revision.

Specimen question

'The main reason for Hitler's growing support was the unpopularity of the Weimar governments.' Do you agree? Explain your answer fully.

[15 marks]

Hints

As usual in questions such as this you need to show that other factors too were at work. If the unpopularity of the government was the most important factor, why didn't people vote Communist? They opposed Weimar too. So there must have been positive reasons. Hitler's patriotism? Hitler's confidence – compare Roosevelt? Hitler's skill as an orator, his use of the media, the slick organisation of his meetings, etc.

The 1932 elections

The 1932 elections were very violent.

Source A

'*There were between 1st June and 20th July in Prussia … 322 serious clashes involving 72 deaths and 497 injured. Prominent socialists and communists were surprised at night and murdered in their beds or shot down at the doors of their houses. The windows of shops owned by Jews were smashed and their contents looted whilst attacks with high explosives were directed against the offices of democratically-owned newspapers.*'

Sir Horace Rumbold, British Ambassador in Berlin: Dispatch to the British Foreign Office, 1932

Source B

Police in a public hall following an election meeting

Specimen questions

1. Study Sources A and B. Which of the two is more convincing evidence that the 1932 elections were violent? Explain your answer.

[5 marks]

Hints

Who wrote Source A? Were the figures he quoted likely to be reliable. Remember it was an important official document, written to tell his government what was going on in Germany. What does Source B prove? Might, for instance, the police have moved in to prevent disorder and cleared the hall? How much does a photograph of one incident tell you about the situation in the country as a whole?

2. What evidence is there in Source A that Hitler's supporters were responsible for much of the violence he described? [5 marks]

check

that you understand how Hitler came to be Chancellor.

Hitler becomes Führer

The Reichstag fire

Once he had become Chancellor, Hitler decided to hold a fresh election in March 1933 to try to win more seats. On 27 February the Reichstag building in Berlin was burnt to the ground. A young Dutch Communist, Marianus van der Lubbe was arrested on the spot and later executed for the crime.

After the fire Hitler claimed that it proved that the Communists were planning to take over the state. He proclaimed a state of emergency giving himself wide powers. He imprisoned anti-Nazis and censored anti-Nazi newspapers. In the election the Nazis won 330 out of 647 seats.

Source

THE REICHSTAG IN FLAMES

Set alight by the Communists! This is what the whole country would look like if Communism and its ally Social Democracy were to come to power only for a few months!

Innocent citizens shot as hostages!

Farmers' houses burnt down!

All Germany must join the outcry:

Stamp Out Communism!

Smash Social Democracy!

VOTE FOR HITLER

Nazi election leaflet (1933)

Specimen questions

1. In what ways was the leaflet misleading? [5 marks]

2. What impression does it give of Hitler's aims? [4 marks]

3. Why was it that many of Hitler's opponents claimed that the Nazis burned down the Reichstag building themselves? [6 marks]

On 23 March the Reichstag passed an Enabling Act giving Hitler absolute power by 441 votes to 94.

The Night of the Long Knives 1934

Hitler's uniformed storm troopers – the SA (*Sturmabtailung*) – had helped him in his campaign to become Chancellor by policing his meetings, beating up his opponents, collecting money and organising marches and demonstrations. By 1934 there were 3 million of them. Their commander was Ernst Roehm.

German army officers hated the SA. In 1934 President Hindenburg was dying, and Hitler wanted to take over from him. To do this he needed the support of the army. On 30 June (The Night of the Long Knives) on Hitler's orders, about 900 prominent SA members, including Roehm were arrested and shot. In August Hindenburg died and Hitler took over, declaring himself '*Führer*' (Leader) of Germany. From then on he relied on the SS (*Schutzstaffel*) under Heinrich Himmler to enforce his wishes.

Source A

'*Revolution is not a permanent condition ... The ideas in our programme impose an obligation on us not to act like fools and to overthrow everything.*'
Hitler: Speech, July 1933

Source B

'*Are we revolutionaries or aren't we? ... If we're not, then we'll go to the dogs.*'
Ernst Roehm: Interview, 1934

Source C

'The government isn't going to last long. The main thing for me is that I've got work through the SA. I played along till then. Now the SA can go to blazes.'

Gestapo report on an SA member in Essen

Source D

'I swear to thee, Adolf Hitler … Loyalty and Bravery. I vow to thee and to the superiors whom thou shalt appoint obedience unto death, so help me God.'

Oath sworn by SS members

Hints

Policy clashes between Roehm and Hitler? Trustworthiness of SA compared with SS? Remember to refer to the sources in your answer.

Specimen question

What evidence is there in the timetable that Hitler had a continuing trust in Himmler?

[4 marks]

Specimen question

Read the sources. In what ways do they add to the account of the reasons for the Night of the Long Knives given in the text?   [10 marks]

check

that you understand how Hitler became Führer.

The rise of Himmler and the SS timetable

1925 Schutzstaffel (SS) set up within the SA to guard Nazi leaders.

1929 SS numbered about 200. Himmler put in charge.

1933 Himmler put in charge of secret police over most of Germany. Set up first concentration camp at Dachau. The SS later administered all the 'death camps'.

1934 SS had 50,000 members. Made independent of SA. Himmler put in charge of Gestapo (Prussian secret police).

1936 All German criminal police merged with secret police under Himmler.

1939 Himmler appointed 'Commissioner for strengthening German Folkdom' i.e. eliminating Jews.

1940 Waffen (armed) SS set up to fight under Himmler's control. Eventually numbered 600,000 men.

1943 Himmler and SS put in charge of the German rocket programme.

The German economy 1933–9

Hitler believed that the Germans were the master race. So he was determined to create a strong, stable, independent and beautiful country for them to live in and to make sure that they all had work with enough pay for them to live pleasant and prosperous lives. The Mind Map will remind you of Hitler's economic policies.

Notes

The LSO was the Labour Service Organisation which provided work for school leavers building sea walls, draining marshes and other such jobs.

Autarchy means that a country produces everything that it needs, not having to rely on imports. Hitler wanted Germany to achieve this. He did not succeed.

Source A

Economic statistics

Production percentages				
	1928	1932	1935	1938
Coal	100	69	95	123
Steel	100	33	109	154
Chemicals	100	51	79	127
Household goods	100	70	80	114

Unemployment (millions)	
1932	5.6
1933	4.8
1934	2.7
1935	2.2
1936	1.6
1937	0.9
1938	0.4

A 'Strength Through Joy' poster advertising cheap travel for German workers. The caption reads 'Now you too can travel'.

Source C

'He [Hitler] is a great and wonderful leader. He is the saviour of Germany.'

David Lloyd George: interview, 1936

Source D

'[In 1951] almost half of those citizens of the Federal Republic of Germany questioned in a public opinion survey described the period between 1933 and 1939 as one in which things had gone best for Germany.'

Ulrich Herbert: *Life in the Third Reich* (1987)

Specimen question

'The information in Sources A, B and C is enough to account for the happy memories of Germany in the 1930s mentioned in Source D.' Do you agree? Explain your answer fully. [12 marks]

Hints

To get good marks you need to analyse what the sources show and use your own knowledge to indicate what they leave out.

Model answer

The sources show that after 1933 the German economy steadily improved. Source A shows that industrial production grew, until by 1938 it was more than in 1928 in all sectors. At the same time unemployment was falling steadily to less than half a million in 1938. Source B shows that the government made sure that workers benefited, laying on opportunities for travel never before available to ordinary working people. Source C shows that in Hitler they had a leader who was admired by visiting statesmen. All these things might be remembered with pleasure.

But other changes, not mentioned in the sources, also appealed to the German people. The sources do not mention agriculture. Hitler made sure that the incomes of farmers increased. Law and order is also left out. For most Germans law and order was much better maintained than it had been under Weimar. Finally, the sources do not say anything about foreign policy. Hitler's decisions to leave the League of Nations, begin to re-arm, enter the Rhineland and unite with Austria in spite of the Treaty of Versailles were all very popular. So though the information in the sources helps to account for the happy memories, the sources don't tell the whole story.

check

that you understand how the German economy improved under Hitler.

Life under the Nazis

Keeping control

The Mind Map will remind you of the methods used by Hitler to keep control of Germany.

The law

Hitler controlled the law. He could make new laws by decree, and if he did not like the way a court was working he abolished it and replaced it by another.

Source A

'The Law and the Führer are one.'

H Göring to a meeting of Prussian lawyers in 1934

'Say to yourselves at every decision which you make: "How would the Führer decide in my place?"'

Dr Hans Frank, Commissioner of Justice, to a conference of judges in 1936

Source B

'As the prisoner refused to give information he was tortured ... He was held by three assistants while the official and another assistant took turns in beating him with a flexible leather-covered steel rod. When he fainted from pain and loss of blood he was brought to by means of various other tortures.'

Account of a Gestapo office in Hamburg: *Manchester Guardian*, 1 July 1935

Specimen questions

1 How did the Nazi system of justice ensure that Hitler's wishes were carried out? [6 marks]

2 What evidence is there that the Nazis believed their system of law was one to be proud of? [5 marks]

Hint

Is there any evidence in the sources that they tried to conceal it? Or did they boast about it?

check

that you understand how the Nazis administered the law.

Hitler Youth timetable

1933	Rival youth groups except church groups banned.
1935	Civil servants ordered to send their children to Hitler Youth.
1936	Church youth groups banned.
1939	All young people ordered to join Hitler Youth.

Hitler Youth

Source A

'All of the German youth in the Reich is organised within the Hitler Youth … The German Youth shall be educated physically, intellectually and morally in the spirit of National Socialism … through the Hitler Youth.'

Adolf Hitler: Decree, December 1936

Source B

The diagram shows Hitler Youth activities.

Source C

'In the presence of this blood banner which represents our Führer, I swear to devote all my energies and my strength to the saviour of our country, Adolf Hitler. I am willing and ready to give up my life for him, so help me God.'

Oath taken by Hitler Youth boys

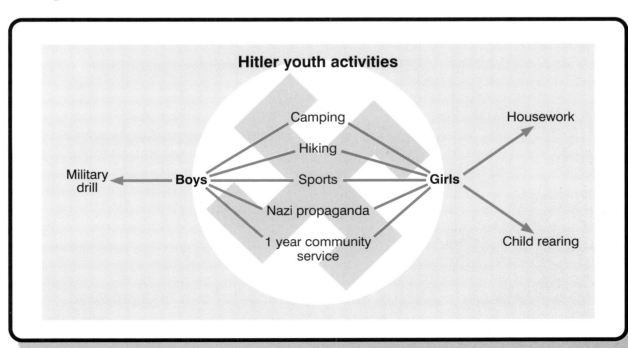

Hitler youth activities

6

Source D

'No one in our class ever read Mein Kampf. *I myself only took quotations from the book. On the whole we didn't know very much about ideology … Nevertheless we were politically programmed: to obey orders, to cultivate the soldierly "virtue" of standing to attention and saying "Yes, Sir" and to stop thinking when the magic word "Fatherland" was uttered.'*

An anonymous German quoted in Detler Peukert: *Youth in the Third Reich* (1987)

Source E

'I was sent for my period of Community Service to a camp in East Prussia. This time was the most carefree of my life. During the harvesting we used to work more than fifteen hours a day. We were so tired I could hardly stand up. But I was so happy because I felt useful. Among us there were country girls, students, hairdressers, domestic servants.'

Melita Maschmann in *The Encyclopaedia of the Second World War*

Specimen questions

1 What evidence is there that Nazis believed that the Hitler Youth movement would strengthen Hitler's hold on Germany?

[5 marks]

2 To what extent does Source D cast doubt on the effectiveness of the Hitler Youth programme? [6 marks]

Hints

How typical might his reaction have been? Did the fact that he did not know much about ideology matter so long as he did what he was told?

3 Girls' activities in Hitler Youth differed in some ways from those of boys. Explain the difference. [4 marks]

4 To what extent does Source E show that Hitler Youth was a force for good? [10 marks]

Hints

Ten marks demands an extended answer, perhaps along these lines: The extract might show that some aspects of Hitler Youth were good – give examples, but other aspects were not – give examples. Then balance the two.

Schools

Hitler reformed the German school system:

1 All **teachers** had to promise to be 'loyal and obedient to Adolf Hitler'.

2 The number of **girls** allowed into higher education was drastically cut.

3 In **History** pupils learned that Germans were the master race, and that the Jews caused all the evil in the world.

4 In **Biology** they learned that it was vital to keep the German race pure.

5 In **Physics** and **Chemistry** they ignored discoveries made by Jewish scientists.

6 Pupils spent hours studying *Mein Kampf*.

7 Hitler set up special schools, concentrating on competitive sports, to educate future leaders.

Make your own Mind Map of Hitler's school reforms

Specimen question

What effect would you expect the reforms to have on scientific knowledge and research in Germany? Explain your answer. [4 marks]

check

that you understand how the Hitler Youth movement worked.

Hitler's opponents

When Hitler came to power in 1933 he was opposed by democratic political parties and by the Communists.

Source A

'The sole political party existing in Germany is the National Socialist German Workers' Party … Whoever shall undertake to maintain the organisation of another party, or to start a new party shall be punished with a sentence of hard labour of up to three years.'

Law Against the New Formation of Parties, 14 July 1933

Source B

(A lawyer's client was tried and found not guilty under the 14 July law)

'He was just in time to see his client being marched away between two uniformed guards and bundled into a green van … [His] client had vanished without trace.'

C Bielenberg (the lawyer's wife): *The Past is Myself* (1984)

Source C

This table lists some of Hitler's opponents in Germany, shows why they opposed him and what happened to them. The list is not complete.

Source D

[At the end of 1944] *'the fact seems beyond dispute – the great proportion of the German people still believed in Adolf Hitler.'*

General Heinz Guderian: *Panzer Leader* (1952)

Specimen questions

1 Why was there no organised political opposition to Hitler after 1933?   [5 marks]

Hints

Remember to refer to both sources (A and B) in your answer.

2 Do you think the lawyer (Source B) was running a risk in defending his client? Explain your answer.   [4 marks]

Hints

Consider his status as a lawyer on the one hand, as against the ruthlessness of the Nazis on the other.

Socialists and Communists	Opposed most of Hitler's policies.	Camps, prisons, executions
Trade Unionists	Wanted to organise workers independently of the Nazis.	Camps, prisons, executions
Ernst Roehm	Leader of the SA. Wanted a more revolutionary policy (1934).	Killed (Night of Long Knives)
Martin Niemöller	Protestant Pastor. Opposed Nazification of Church.	Concentration camp 1937–45
'July' Generals	Tried to assassinate Hitler to end war in 1944.	About 4,900 executed or killed themselves
Dietrich Bonhoeffer	Lutheran Pastor. Joined July conspiracy.	Executed 1945

Specimen question

3 Does the fate of Hitler's opponents outlined in Source C account for the German people's professed support for Hitler as reported in Source D? Explain your answer fully.

[15 marks]

Hints

As always, suspect the offer of one, simple explanation. In this case you could point out that the statement in the source that they 'believed in' Hitler contradicts the view that they only supported him out of fear. Also, consider: Gratitude for his past achievements (mention some), the effect of propaganda, patriotic support for the leader in wartime, the lack of any alternative leader.

check

that you understand why the opposition to Hitler failed.

The impact of war

Re-armament

In 1936 Hitler ordered Göring to launch a four-year plan to re-arm in preparation for a large-scale war beginning any time after 1940.

In 1942 Hitler put Albert Speer in charge of the German armaments industry. Production increased.

Source A

Financial statistics (billions of marks)		
	Spent on re-armament	Size of National Debt
1935	5.4	15.9
1936	10.2	20.1
1937	10.9	25.8
1938	17.2	31.2

Source B

'With the extension of the period of compulsory military service to two years on 24 August 1936, the constitution of military works ... and, beginning in 1938–39 the addition of naval re-armament to the army and air force programmes, the situation became so acute as to necessitate the direction of labour.'

K Hildebrand: *The Third Reich* (1984)

Source C

'The construction of the navy as ordered by me, must have priority over all other tasks in armaments including those of the other two branches of the armed forces.'

Adolf Hitler: Directive in January 1939

Source D

'When the German army attacked Russia in 1941 only a third of the force was fully equipped with German arms. Most of the rest had some equipment captured from France and Czechoslovakia or else were short of some of their weapons.'

John Patrick: *Hindsight* (1995)

Specimen questions

1 Study Source A. How did the Nazi government pay for increased re-armament before 1939? [2 marks]

2 What evidence is there in Sources B and C that the arms drive was poorly organised? [4 marks]

3 Had Göring fulfilled Hitler's order to prepare for a large-scale war by 1940? Explain your answer. [5 marks]

Life in wartime

The Mind Map will show you the effects of the war on life in Germany. Remember that conditions gradually got worse as the war went on.

Goods and people from conquered countries were brought back to Germany during the war.

'Whenever you come across anything that may be needed by the German people you must be after it like a bloodhound. It must be … brought to Germany.'

H Göring: Instruction quoted in the Nuremburg war crime trials

Source B

'The Slavs are here to work for us. In so far as we don't need them, they may die.'

Martin Bormann, Hitler's deputy: Letter, 1942

Source C

'They … went about in their bare feet. The sole clothing of each consisted of a sack with holes for their arms and head … The amount of food in their camp was extremely meagre and of very poor quality. One could not enter their barracks without being attacked by fleas.'

Dr Wilhelm Jaeger: Evidence at the Nuremburg trials on foreign workers at a wartime Krupps munitions factory

Specimen questions

1. What does Source A tell us about the Nazi leaders' attitude to the people of the occupied countries? [3 marks]

2. What do Sources B and C tell us about their attitude to those working in forced labour camps? [4 marks]

3. How might the Nazis have justified their point of view? [4 marks]

Hint

Think about Nazi racial theories.

check

that you understand how life in Germany changed in wartime.

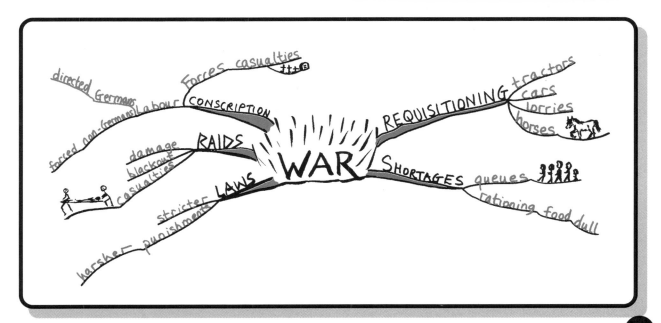

Hitler and the Jews

All his life Hitler hated Jews. Once he was in power he began to harass them.

It is generally agreed that by the end of the war the Nazis had killed about 6 million Jews, 2.5 million of whom came from Poland.

Source A

'Above all, I charge the leaders of the nation and those under them to … merciless opposition to the universal poisoner of all peoples, international Jewry.'

Hitler: *Political Testament* (April 1945)

Source B

'I saw the crematorium and realised for the first time that things like that do exist, because we have heard a lot of stories of those things but … you just can't realise it can be true and you thought, "Well, not really, people exaggerate" … But this was the first time that it hit home that it's true and the chances are that you will get killed.'

Concentration camp survivor: BBC documentary

Specimen questions

1 What evidence convinced the speaker in Source B that his life was in danger?

[2 marks]

2 After the war many Germans claimed that they did not know that extermination camps existed. Does this seem likely? Refer to Source B and to your own knowledge.

[6 marks]

3 Some historians claim that Hitler would not have approved of the extermination of the Jews. Does Source A disprove this view?

[6 marks]

Jewish persecution timetable

1933 Government organised boycott of Jewish shops, lawyers and doctors.

1935 All official positions barred to non-Germans. 'Mixed' marriages forbidden.

1937 Some Jewish businesses confiscated.

1938 **April** Jewish wealth registered

June Jewish businesses registered.

Oct 17,000 Jews expelled from Germany.

Nov 'Crystal Night': 7,500 Jewish shops destroyed, 400 synagogues burnt down; 20,000 Jews imprisoned. Jewish pupils excluded from schools.

Dec Jewish businesses and valuables confiscated.

1939 Jews ordered to live in special Jewish houses.

1940 Wholesale deportation of Jews began.

1942 Massed gassing of Jews began at Auschwitz.

Hints

You need a lot of evidence to disprove a view. First, is the source likely to represent Hitler's real views? When was it written? Why? Is it consistent with what he wrote or said at other times? Next, does what he wrote amount to approval of the extermination of the Jews?

check

that you understand how the Nazis tried to exterminate the Jews.

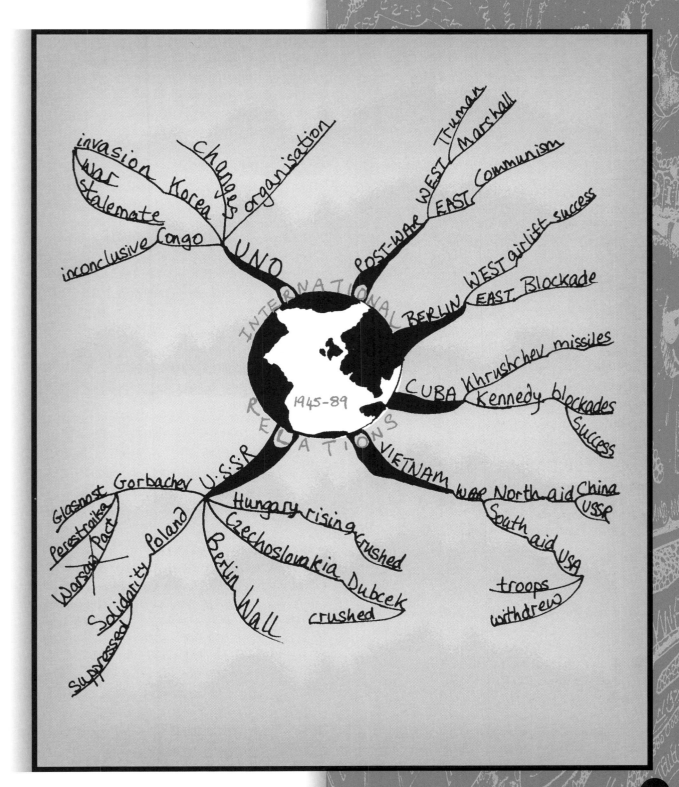

preview
What you need to know

- **How relations between the USSR and its wartime allies got worse between 1945 and 1955**

- **How the Soviet government sited nuclear missiles in Cuba, and how the US government persuaded the USSR to remove them**

- **How the USA became involved in the war in Vietnam, and how they withdrew**

- **The growing unrest in the Eastern Bloc countries following the death of Stalin in 1953**

- **Why the United Nations was founded, how it was organised, how it has changed and how it acted in Korea and the Congo**

The beginning of the Cold War

The Iron Curtain

During the war at conferences at Teheran (1943), Yalta (1945) and Potsdam (1945) the Allied leaders agreed that the Soviet Union should continue to control Eastern Europe after the war, and that Germany should be divided between the four Allies – Britain, France, the USA and the USSR.

The Soviet Union set up communist governments in all the countries they controlled (*see* map).

Source A

'You had the state planning system everywhere … You had communist parties … central committees, Politbureaux, Stalin pictures. You had the same party education materials.'

Wolfgang Leonhard, East German Communist Party official: BBC documentary, 1985

Source B

'From Stettin in the Baltic to Trieste in the Adriatic, an iron curtain has descended across the continent. Behind this line … famous cities and the population around them lie in what I must call the Soviet sphere … Communist fifth columns are established and work in complete unity and absolute obedience to the directions they receive from the Communist centre.'

Winston Churchill: Speech, Fulton Missouri, 1946

Specimen questions

1. Why do you think Churchill called the frontier between the Soviet sphere and Western Europe 'an iron curtain'? [2 marks]

2. Which part of Churchill's speech does Source A seem to support? Explain your answer. [4 marks]

The Marshall Plan

President Truman of the USA feared that the USSR intended to take over the whole of Europe. So in 1947, by the Truman Doctrine, he promised that the USA would help any country threatened by the USSR and, by the Marshall Plan, the USA promised to pay $5,000 million a year to help to strengthen friendly countries including, if they wished, the Soviet Union.

'An iron curtain has descended'

Legend:
- Communist states dominated by USSR
- Communist but neutral
- European states in NATO
- The Iron Curtain

Source A

'Our policy is not directed against any country or doctrine, but against hunger, poverty, desperation and chaos. Its purpose should be the revival of ... political and social conditions in which free institutions can exist.'

General George Marshall: Speech, June 1947

Source B

'The American imperialists ... have taken the path of outright expansion, of enslaving the weakened capitalist states ... They have chosen the path of hatching new war plans against the Soviet Union and the new democracies ... The clearest expression of the policy is provided by the Truman–Marshall plans.'

Georgi Malenkov, Soviet Deputy Prime Minister: Speech, 1947

115

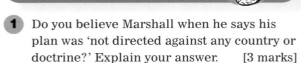

Specimen questions

1 Do you believe Marshall when he says his plan was 'not directed against any country or doctrine?' Explain your answer.　　[3 marks]

Hint

Would Marshall have thought of a communist government as a 'free institution'?

2 What did Malenkov say was the real aim of the Marshall Plan? How could he have justified this view?　　[3 marks]

The Berlin blockade 1948

When Germany and the city of Berlin were divided into occupation zones at the end of the war, everyone took it for granted that a peace treaty would soon be signed and the occupation would end. But by 1948 the four former Allies were on such bad terms that there was no chance of a treaty. So the British and American governments began to unite their zones. In 1948 they tried to persuade the USSR to agree that the two zones could use the same currency. The Russians refused. The British and Americans went ahead anyway.

In June 1948 the USSR closed the road, rail and canal links between West Germany and Berlin. They had blockaded the city. The Allies supplied Berlin by air (*see* map). A cargo plane landed on average every two minutes. On 12 May, 1949, the Russians re-opened the road, railway and canal.

Source A

'*War has left Russia with deep concern about German aggression. They are determined to stop the growth of a strong and possibly hostile Germany in the future.*'

US Ambassador in Moscow: Dispatch, 1947

Specimen question

Read Source A. What evidence is there that fear may have driven the Soviet Union to blockade Berlin? Explain your answer.　　[5 marks]

Occupied Germany from 1945

Hamburg
THE NETHERLANDS　Hanover　Berlin　POLAND
British Zone　Soviet Zone
BELGIUM
FRANCE
LUXEMBOURG　French　Frankfurt　CZECHOSLOVAKIA
Zone　American Zone
Zone
0　100　200 km
SWITZERLAND　AUSTRIA　HUNGARY

France
Great Britain
United States
Soviet Union
Air corridor

Hints

Use your knowledge of events leading up to the blockade as well as the source. Who was the writer? Was he likely to have known the hopes and fears of the Soviet government? Had anything happened which might have led them to think that a strong German state was about to be set up?

Source B

'There was no real choice. Either we did it, or West Berlin was lost to us. We were fairly sure that the Russians didn't want a show-down at that time – not sufficiently recovered from the war, but you can never be sure about that kind of thing, and we certainly weren't at that time.'

Clement Attlee, British Prime Minister, speaking in 1955

Source C

'We have lost Czechoslovakia … We retreat from Berlin? When Berlin falls, Western Germany will be next?'

US General L Clay, speaking in 1948

Specimen question

What evidence is there in Sources B and C that the Western powers felt that they were forced to set up an air lift? Explain your answer. [5 marks]

Model answer

Attlee, who was British Prime Minister at the time, is quoted as saying that the Allies had 'no real choice' because otherwise they would have lost West Berlin. General Clay goes further. He thought that if, following the installation of a Communist government in Czechoslovakia, they lost West Berlin, then they would be turned out of Western Germany. These two opinions, one from the USA and one from Britain are good evidence

that both governments felt they had no choice, but had to mount the air lift.

Source D

THE BIRD WATCHER

A cartoon from *Punch*, July 1948

Specimen question

What does Source D tell us about the Berlin air lift? To what extent is it backed up by the other sources? [8 marks]

Hint

The examiners realise that a cartoon like this may give different messages to different people. They will remember this when marking the answers. But to get good marks you need to link the points you make to details in the cartoon.

Model answer

The cartoon shows that Berlin received its supplies, even bulky, heavy items such as coal, from the air. It shows how vulnerable the air lift was. The aircraft, represented by the slow, delicate birds carrying their bundles, could easily have been shot down by the USSR, represented by Stalin, shown with his gun half-raised, as if in doubt what to do. This backs up the point made by Attlee in Source B that, at the time, people weren't absolutely sure that the Russians didn't want a showdown, so that the decision to use the air lift was risky.

Source E

'We demonstrated to the people of Europe that with their co-operation we would act ... resolutely when their freedom was threatened.'

President Truman: *Memoirs* (1955)

Specimen question

What advantages did the Western Powers get out of the air lift? [4 marks]

Hint

Use your knowledge as well as the source. What effect did the air lift have on the prestige of the USSR? Was this an advantage to the West?

The aftermath of the air lift

The Mind Map will remind you of the results of the air lift.

check

that you understand how the Communist takeover of Eastern Europe, the Truman Doctrine, the Marshall Plan and the Berlin blockade upset relations between the USSR and the West.

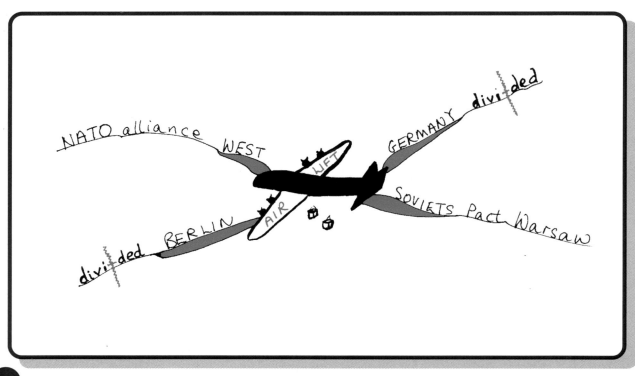

The Cuban Missile Crisis

In the autumn of 1962 the Soviet government, under Nikita Khrushchev, began to build missile sites in Cuba, and shipped nuclear missiles out to them.

Tables like this are a useful way of putting events in order briefly and clearly. Try to compile your own to help your revision.

Specimen question

Why in 1962 might Khrushchev have felt confident enough to challenge Kennedy over Cuba?

[4 marks]

Lead-up to the crisis timetable

1957 USSR launched Sputnik. Boost for USSR.

1958 Khrushchev threatened to hand Berlin over to East Germany as a 'free city'. Alarmed the West.

1959 Castro overthrew US backed Cuban dictator. Asked for aid. USA refused, USSR agreed.

1961 Berlin Wall built. USSR more secure.

USSR sent man into space. Boost for USSR.

Bay of Pigs. Cuban exiles from USA landed on Cuba. Defeated. USSR stepped up aid.

Source A

The area threatened by the missiles based in Cuba

Source B

'I decided to install missiles … with nuclear warheads in Cuba without letting the United States find out until it was too late to do anything about them. The missiles would stop the United States taking any action against Cuba.'

Nikita Khrushchev: *Khrushchev on Khrushchev* (1990)

Source C

'The presence of these large, long-range and clearly offensive weapons … constitutes an explicit threat to the peace and security of all the Americas … This action also contradicts the repeated assurances … that the Soviet Union had no need or desire to station strategic missiles on the territory of any other nation.'

US President Kennedy: Broadcast, 22 October 1962

Source D

'Your rockets are stationed in Turkey … Turkey lies next to us … Do you believe that you have the right to demand … the removal of such weapons that you qualify as offensive while not recognising the right for us?'

Nikita Khrushchev: Message to President Kennedy, 26 October 1962

Specimen questions

1 Why was President Kennedy alarmed that Khrushchev had placed missiles in Cuba? [4 marks]

2 Is there good evidence in the sources that Khrushchev deliberately deceived Kennedy over his plans to put missiles in Cuba? Explain your answer. [5 marks]

3 Could the Soviet rockets in Cuba be fairly compared with US rockets in Turkey? (Source D). Explain your answer. [5 marks]

Hint

Remember you can use your own knowledge of the topic as well as the sources to answer this.

Source E

'All ships of any kind bound for Cuba from whatever nation or port will, if found to contain cargoes of offensive weapons, be turned back … We will call for the prompt dismantling and withdrawal of all offensive weapons in Cuba … before the quarantine can be lifted.'

President Kennedy: Broadcast, 22 October 1962

Source F

'During the seventeen years that have passed since the end of World War 2 there has never been a more dangerous or closer confrontation of the major powers.'

U Thant, UN Secretary General: Statement to UN on 24 October 1962

Specimen questions

1 Why, do you think, did U Thant think that the situation was so dangerous? [3 marks]

Hint

Think of what might have happened as a result of the action outlined in Source E.

2 Why did President Kennedy take the steps outlined in Source E? [10 marks]

Hint

The way to answer this question must depend on how many marks are on offer. A few marks demand a simple answer. Don't waste time giving more. But 10+ marks need careful thought.

If Kennedy had done nothing, what would the effects have been on his prestige in the USA, on the safety of the USA, on his allies, on the prestige of the USSR? If he had done more (e.g. sink the ships, bomb the missile sites) what might Khrushchev have done to retaliate? Nuclear war? So Kennedy compromised.

'We sent the Americans a note saying we agreed to remove our missiles … on condition that the President assured us that there would be no invasion of Cuba. Finally Kennedy gave in and agreed to [give] … such an assurance. It was a great victory for us.'

Nikita Khrushchev: *Khrushchev on Khrushchev* (1990)

'In the Communist world [Khrushchev] suffered a blow to his prestige from which he was never really to recover. His judgement was called into question in every Communist capital including his own.'

Geoffrey Stern, (Lecturer in International Relations): BBC documentary, 1985

Specimen question

Khrushchev claimed that the Cuban Missile Crisis was 'a great victory'. So why did Geoffrey Stern say it was a blow to his prestige? Explain your answer.   [10 marks]

Hints

Note the reason Khrushchev gives in Source B for placing rockets in Cuba. Did he fulfil this aim? But was this his real aim? If it was not, then what was? Humiliation for the USA? Prestige for the USSR? Who backed down in the end?

Aftermath

The Mind Map will remind you of the results of the Cuban Missile Crisis.

check

that you can explain why Khrushchev may have wanted to place rockets on Cuba, why Kennedy acted as he did, and what the results were.

The Vietnam War 1964–75

Background

Vietnam was part of Indo-China, which used to be a French colony. In 1954 the French were driven out by the Vietcong, a Communist guerrilla group. At the 1954 Geneva conference Indo-China was divided into four. Laos and Cambodia were to be independent countries. North Vietnam, ruled by the Communists, and South Vietnam, ruled by a right-wing dictator, were to be united after free elections. Diem, the dictator supported by the USA, refused to hold elections. Why was the USA interested?

Source A

'We'd never heard of the place before … The country was absolutely blank on the whole subject of Vietnam. And therefore the more easily could we impose on it the ideas we had in mind about the Cold War and the necessity of fighting the evil of Communism.'

Professor Fairbank, A US foreign policy expert: BBC documentary, 1985

Source B

'If … Vietnam became … Communist … then it would probably be used as an effective base for further subversion outward and [surrounding countries] … would … tend to come under domination one at a time.'

Robert Bowie, US State Department official: BBC documentary, 1985

Source C

'The rulers in Hanoi are urged on by Peking. This is a regime which has destroyed freedom in Tibet, which has attacked India, and has been condemned by the United Nations for aggression in Korea. It is a nation which is helping the forces of violence in almost every continent.'

US President Lyndon Johnson: Speech, April 1965

Source D

'The Soviets were utterly opposed to free elections in Germany, utterly opposed to free elections in Korea, so … why should we accommodate them in one spot if they won't accommodate us in these other places?'

Dean Rusk, US Secretary of State: BBC documentary, 1985

Specimen question

1. Study the sources. Do they confirm the view that the US government had no interest in the welfare of the Vietnamese people? Explain your answer. [6 marks]

Hint

This does not ask you just to list all the evidence which supports the view. You have also to look carefully for any evidence on the other side and weigh it against the rest.

2 The US government claimed that the war in Vietnam was a fight for democracy. Do the sources support this view? Explain your answer. [6 marks]

Hint

Look particularly at Source D.

Vietnam timetable

1954–64	US aid to South Vietnam.
1964	Vietminh attacked US ships in Gulf of Tonkin. US sank Vietminh ships.
1965	US air raids on Hanoi. US sent troops to Vietnam.
1966	Over 150 US air raids a day on targets in North and South Vietnam.
1968	Tet offensive – Vietcong attacked nearly 100 towns in South Vietnam, 300 US deaths a week in Vietnam.
	US began air raids on Laos and Cambodia.
	Nixon reduced the number of US troops in Vietnam.
1972	Nixon promised to end war.
1973	Cease fire signed. US troops withdrew.
1975	Vietcong took over South Vietnam

Total US casualties in Vietnam: 57,685 killed, 153,303 wounded.

Vietnamese casualties more than 2 million.

Source A

'JUST GIVE US THE TOOLS AND WE'LL GET THE JOB DONE'
Thurs., July 6, 1967
ST. LOUIS POST-DISPATCH

This cartoon, showing flag-draped US coffins, appeared in a US paper in July 1965

Specimen questions

1 What effect was the cartoon intended to have on readers' attitude to the Vietnam War? [2 marks]

2 Was the cartoon's message accurate? Explain your answer. [4 marks]

'Let us be proud of the two and a half million young Americans who served in Vietnam … with honour and distinction in one of the most selfless enterprises in the history of nations. And let us be proud of those who … gave their lives so that the people of South Vietnam might live in freedom.'

President Nixon: Speech, January 1973

Specimen question

Can President Nixon's view of the US role in Vietnam be justified? Explain your answer.

[10 marks]

Hint

You earn good marks on questions like this by backing up the points you make with valid arguments and good evidence, no matter what view you take.

Model answer

President Nixon was right when he said that Vietnam was a 'selfless' war, because the USA had nothing to gain from it. The US government was fighting to prevent the Communists taking over South East Asia. Many US troops behaved bravely and honourably, but some committed atrocities, such as the Mi Lai massacre, and in any case some US tactics, such as the widespread use of napalm and defoliants, which were bound to damage innocent lives, were controversial. The US government never fought to enable the South Vietnamese to live in freedom. The governments the USA supported were right-wing dictatorships. When he spoke in 1973, on the occasion of signing the cease fire, Nixon had to make an up-beat speech like this, but it is a very one-sided view.

Vietnam aftermath

The Vietnam War caused social conflict in the USA. The failure to prevent the Communist takeover made the USA lose confidence in itself.

Source

'If you want to, go ahead and fight in the jungles of Vietnam. The French fought there for seven years and still had to quit in the end. Perhaps the Americans will be able to stick it out a little longer, but eventually they will have to quit too.'

Khrushchev in a conversation with Dean Rusk in 1961

check

that you understand why, in spite of Khrushchev's warning, the USA got involved in the Vietnam War, and how Khrushchev's prophecy came true.

The Eastern Bloc 1953–89

Background

The Soviet Union controlled Eastern Europe through the Warsaw Pact, signed in 1955. It put all Eastern European armies under Soviet control, and allowed the USSR to station troops in Warsaw Pact countries, which shielded the USSR from an attack from the West (*see* map).

In February 1956 the Russian leader, Khrushchev, made a speech criticising Stalin, who had died in 1953. He said:

'Stalin called people who did not agree with him "enemies of the people". This term allowed him to kill and imprison illegally anyone he wished. People couldn't argue with him.'

This speech made many people in Warsaw Pact countries believe that Khrushchev was in favour of reform and free speech.

The Hungarian Rising 1956

In October 1956 the Hungarian people overthrew their Stalinist leader, Rakosi, and set up Imre Nagy in his place.

The Mind Map on the next page will give you an idea of Nagy's policies.

At first, Khrushchev supported Nagy, and promised to withdraw Soviet troops, but when Nagy said Hungary would leave the Warsaw Pact, Khrushchev sent Soviet tanks into Budapest, overthrew Nagy, and set up Janos Kadar in his place.

Warsaw Pact (1955)
† Albania expelled, 1961

Former Soviet zone

Independent
Communist state

USSR

EAST
GERMANY

POLAND

CZECHOSLOVAKIA

HUNGARY

ROMANIA

YUGOSLAVIA

ALBANIA
†

0   500 km

Specimen questions

1. What changes did Imre Nagy make in Hungary? [4 marks]

2. Why did some of these changes upset the Soviet government? [6 marks]

3. 'The most important lesson of the Hungarian Rising of 1956 was that the Soviet Union was in complete control of its Eastern allies.' Do you agree with this statement? Explain your answer. [10 marks]

Hint

Always suspect phrases like 'most important'. For example, why was there a revolt in Hungary at all if the Soviets were in complete control? Why did Khrushchev allow some of Nagy's reforms? Would it be better to say that the Soviet Union was the final judge of what was acceptable? Another important lesson was that dissident Eastern Bloc countries could not expect any help from the West.

check

Check that you can explain why some Eastern Bloc countries expected more freedom after 1953, and why the Soviet Union acted as it did against Hungary in 1956.

The Prague Spring 1968

In 1968 two new leaders, Alexander Dubcek and Ludovik Svoboda, took control of the Communist Party in Czechoslovakia. They brought in many reforms (*see* Mind Map on the next page).

Source A

'There was a tremendous discrepancy between the theory and the practice ... So I think all what we wanted to do, to find a more honest, more human way to fulfil the aims we have in mind for the last twenty years.'

Y Hanzelka, Czech government spokesman, speaking in 1968

Travel Trade LIBERATED FREED politics speech writing
Communism RETAINED PRAGUE SPRING REFORMED Police
Alliance

1968 timetable

January	Dubcek became General Secretary of Czech Communist Party. Reforms began.
May–June	Soviet army manoeuvres on Czech borders. East German and Soviet press criticised reforms.
July	Meetings between Czech and other Warsaw Pact leaders.
4 August	Agreement reached. Reforms to go ahead.
14 August	Soviet press attacked reforms.
17 August	Brezhnev accused Dubcek of breaking agreement.
20 August	Soviet, East German, Hungarian, Polish and Bulgarian troops invaded Czechoslovakia.

Source B

'The whole atmosphere was exciting. People were free to talk without fear of arrest and to make contact with new ideas, inside or outside Czechoslovakia.'

William Wallace: *Czechoslovakia*

Source C

'[A minister] reported … that Soviet troops along with units from four other Warsaw Pact countries had crossed the borders into Czechoslovakia … Dubcek said, "So they did it after all – and to me".'

Zdenck Mlynav, a Czech Communist Party official: *Night Frost in Prague*

Source D

'All the signposts, street names and name cards on apartment doors disappeared overnight. All the streets were called Dubcek or Svoboda Street. All the towns were named Dubcekov or Svobodov'

Ladislav Mnacko: *The Seventh Night*

Source E

'It was very hard coming down from the exhilaration of the changes. You suddenly found yourself completely helpless, crashing down to complete despair.'

Czech civilian looking back on 1968: BBC documentary, 1985

7

Specimen questions

1 What evidence is there that Dubcek's government genuinely did not want to upset the Soviet Union? [5 marks]

Hints

Compare his reforms with those of Imry Nagy in Hungary in 1956. Look at the timetable. Look at Source C.

2 Is there any evidence that the USSR and its allies found it difficult to agree to invade Czechoslovakia? Explain your answer.

[4 marks]

Hint

Look at the 1968 timetable.

3 What evidence is there that the Czech people supported Dubcek's reforms? [4 marks]

4 Explain why the five powers eventually decided to crush the Czech reforms. [6 marks]

Hints

The answer to question 4 is not in the sources. Perhaps demand for reforms might spread? Might existing leaders lose power? Might Communism be undermined? Might the Warsaw pact be undermined? Might the Warsaw Pact disintegrate? Was it too risky?

check

that you understand why the USSR and its allies invaded Czechoslovakia

The Prague Spring aftermath

The Soviet Union lost prestige. The Soviets were criticised by China, Albania and Romania as well as by all the Western powers.

The Berlin Wall

Background

The USA, Britain and France controlled part of the city of Berlin and had the right to travel to it through East Germany. West Berlin was a shop-window for the West. It was very prosperous and had fewer restrictions than the East. What was more, it provided an easy route for East Germans who wanted to live in the West. The Soviet Union and East Germany tried to solve this problem in various ways.

Berlin timetable

1948 Tried to force Western Powers out by blockade. Foiled by air lift.

1958 Khrushchev proposed to hand East Berlin over to the East Germans. West vetoed idea.

1959 140,000 East Germans left through West Berlin.

1960 200,000 East Germans left through West Berlin.

1961 Jan–June: 100,000 East Germans left through West Berlin.

Khrushchev wanted to hand over all border controls to East Germans. West refused.

August: Eastern forces built the Berlin Wall sealing off West Berlin. West protested.

1963 President Kennedy visited Berlin. He said, *'There are those who say there is no difference between the East and the West. Let them come to Berlin.'*

Specimen questions

1 Why did the Soviet and East German authorities feel that they had to build the wall in 1961? [4 marks]

Hint

To earn all four marks you will need to mention the particular circumstances of 1961.

2 What advantage did the wall give to the West? [2 marks]

Solidarity in Poland

Background

Most Poles are Roman Catholics. They disliked the atheist Communist governments which had ruled them since 1948. Food was short and life was hard. In 1980 there were a number of strikes organised by Solidarity, a trade union led by Lech Walesa, an electrician. Solidarity signed an agreement with the government. In this agreement the government promised to increase food rations, reduce hours of work, allow freedom of worship and stop censoring the press and broadcasting.

Shortages continued in Poland and in the autumn of 1981 there were more strikes and demonstrations. Advised by the Soviet leader, L Brezhnev, the Polish President, General Jaruzelski, dissolved Solidarity, arrested its leaders and imposed martial law. In 1983 Lech Walesa was awarded the Nobel Peace Prize.

Specimen question

The USSR did not intervene in Poland in 1980. What message would this give to 'reformers' in Eastern Europe? [3 marks]

Hint

Compare with the Prague Spring in 1968.

Source

'If the outrages in Poland do not cease, we cannot and will not conduct business as usual with the perpetrators and those who aid and abet them.'

US President Reagan: Speech, December 1981

Specimen question

What did the USSR lose by its policy towards Poland in 1980 and 1981? Explain your answer. [4 marks]

Hint

Was the policy consistent? Did it give an impression of strength and certainty?

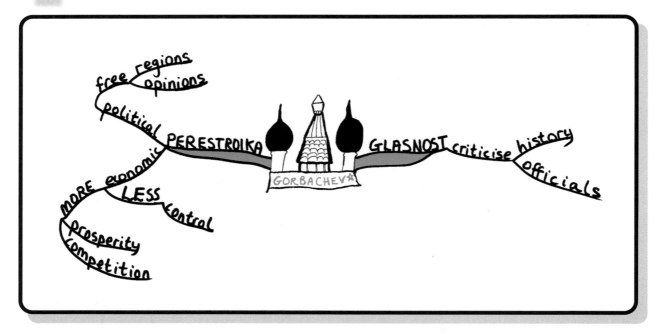

free regions opinions
political PERESTROIKA GLASNOST criticise history officials
MORE economic LESS control
prosperity competition
GORBACHEV

Reform in the USSR 1985–9

In 1985 Mikhail Gorbachev became head of the Soviet government. He wanted to reform the Soviet system. The Mind Map will show you what he wanted to do.

Gorbachev believed that the Soviet Communist Party was strong enough to remain in power after his reforms. He was wrong. The reforms resulted in the collapse of the whole Soviet system in the USSR.

Gorbachev's reforms also affected all the Communist states in Eastern Europe. Gorbachev made it clear that if the people there wanted a different system of government he would not try to prevent it. All the Communist governments were unpopular and inefficient, and in 1989 they all fell from power. Most important, the people of East Germany decided to join up with West Germany in a new united Germany.

Specimen question

Was Gorbachev responsible for the fall of Communism in Eastern Europe? Explain your answer fully. [15 marks]

Hint

Always suspect statements that offer one simple explanation for things. Who appointed Gorbachev? Who helped him to carry out his policies? Why did the peoples of Eastern Europe want to get rid of their governments? Give examples of how they had tried in the past. Mention the growing uncertainty of Soviet policy.

check

that you can explain why the USSR acted against Poland in 1981, why the East Germans and the Soviet Union built the Berlin Wall and why the whole system collapsed in 1989.

The United Nations

The Second World War (1939–45) was incredibly destructive and expensive. World leaders were determined that there must never be another war like it. So in 1945 they set up the United Nations Organisation (UNO) which they hoped would help to keep the peace. They tried to make it stronger than the League of Nations had been.

Organisation

General Assembly
Meets every year. Every member country has one vote. Discusses problems. Makes recommendations, appoints committees.

Security Council
Five great powers are permanent members. Can veto decisions. Others selected by assembly for two years. Job is to preserve peace. Can order members to provide troops to keep the peace.

Central Organisation

Secretariat
Administers UN under the control of the Secretary General, who can raise issues and suggest policies to the assembly and the Security Council.

Specimen questions

1 In what ways was the United Nations stronger than the League of Nations had been?
[4 marks]

Hint

You need to use your knowledge about the League of Nations as well as the source.

2 Under what circumstances might the Security Council be unable to act, even though the majority of members wanted it to? [2 marks]

More members

Since 1945 large numbers of colonies have gained their independence. They have all joined the UN.

Source

'It used to be that the UN reflected the Cold War divisions which were mostly East–West. But … since about 1960 it has become … a forum for North-South encounters. … Now the big subjects are colonialism, sovereignty over natural resources and the evolution of the doctrine that the have-not nations "as a matter of right" are entitled to economic help from the have nations.'

David Popper, US Assistant Secretary of State: Speech, 1973

Specimen questions

1 What evidence is there in the source that:
(a) Before 1960 discussions in the UN Assembly were usually about political disagreements between Communist states and Western democracies?
(b) After 1960 the assembly was more interested in working for equality among the world's peoples? [2 marks]

Hint

The purpose of this question is to check that you understand the source.

2 Do you think this source is reliable? Give reasons for your answer. [5 marks]

Hint

Should somebody in Popper's position have been familiar with what was going on in the UN? Might his view be biased? Might the representative of a 'have-not' country have had a different view?

The Korean War 1950–3

In 1950 Korea was divided into two. North Korea was Communist. South Korea was capitalist. Suddenly, without warning, North Korea invaded South Korea.

Source A

'I would be grateful …. if your governments would consider the possibility of assistance … including combat forces [to repel the invasion]'

Trygve Lie, UN Secretary General: Letter to the Security Council, 1950

Source B

'What is happening … is important to every American …. This attack has made it clear beyond all doubt that the international Communist movement is willing to use armed invasion to conquer independent nations.'

US President Truman: Speech, 1950

Source C

'If the aggressor gets away with it, aggressors all over the world will be encouraged. The same results which led to the Second World War will follow and another World War may result'

Clement Attlee, UK Prime Minister: Speech, 1950

Specimen questions

1 Do you think President Truman's claim regarding the 'international Communist movement' was justified? Explain your answer. [4 marks]

Hints

Was there such a thing as the 'international Communist movement'? Was North Korea acting with the advice and consent of China and the USSR?

2 What do you think Clement Attlee hoped to achieve by supporting Trygve Lie? [4 marks]

USSR boycott

When the invasion took place the USSR was boycotting the UN Security Council to protest against the fact that China's place on the Council had been given to the Nationalists, who only ruled Formosa, instead of the Communists, who ruled the whole of China.

In the absence of the USSR the Council agreed to Trygve Lie's request, and 16 countries sent troops to Korea to fight against the North. During the war 400,000 UN and 1.6 million Communist servicemen were killed or injured. Huge numbers of civilians were killed, injured and made homeless.

Korean timetable

1950	**June–September:**	Communist forces occupied all Korea except for an area around Pusan.
	September–November:	UN troops drove North Korean forces back to the Chinese frontier.
	November:	Chinese forces attacked the UN forces and drove them back into South Korea.
1951		UN forces drove Chinese back to about the 38th Parallel. Negotiations for armistice began.
1953		Armistice signed. Frontier between North and South fixed along the 38th Parallel.

The maps show what happened in visual form. Notice how much information can be crammed on to a map. Try drawing your own to help with your revision.

June–November 1950

◄═══ North Korean attack 25 June–15 September 1950

◄─── UN counter-attack 15 September–
26 October 1950

------ UN front line with dates

CHINA

Yalu R.

NORTH KOREA

26 October 1950

•Pyongyang

38th Parallel

•Seoul

15 September

30 September

SOUTH KOREA

Yellow Sea

Area held by UN
throughout
the war

•Pusan

November 1950–1

◄═══ Chinese/North Korean offensive
26 October 1950–22 April 1951

◄─── UN repulse of Chinese/North Korean attack

─── Furthest Chinese/North Korean advance

CHINA

Yalu R.

NORTH
KOREA

Pyongyang •

38th Parallel

Final armistice line
26 December 1950

•Seoul

25 January 1951

Yellow Sea

SOUTH KOREA

Area held by UN
throughout
the war

•Pusan

Specimen question

Was the Korean War a success for the UN?
Explain your answer.   [10 marks]

Hints

The North Koreans were driven back. But the
quarrel between North and South was not settled.
Action was possible only because the USSR was
not present in the Security Council. The UN had
to rely on a US general and the US army
organisation. In the end the US took over the war.
Conclusion?

7

The Congo Crisis 1960–5

Congo timetable

1960	**June**	Belgium granted Congo its independence under President Kasavubu and Prime Minister Lumumba.
	July	Moise Tshombe declared Katanga, a rich mining area, independent under his rule. The UN voted to send in troops.
1961	**Jan**	Katangan troops captured and killed Lumumba.
	Aug	Katangan troops attacked UN forces.
	Sept	UN Secretary General Hammarskjold killed in air crash on Congo borders.
1963		Tshombe fled to Europe. Katanga reunited with Congo.
1964	**Jan**	UN forces left.
	July	Tshombe returned. Made Prime Minister. War continued.
1965		General Mobutu took control in a coup d'état.

Specimen question

How successful was the UN in the Congo?

[6 marks]

Hints

Hammarskjold showed how the Assembly, where there was no veto, could by-pass the Security Council. But what happened to the imposed settlement once the UN troops left? And how was the crisis eventually settled?

Conclusion?

check

Go back over the section on the United Nations and draw up your own Mind Map on the organisation and work of the UNO.

8 China 1911–90

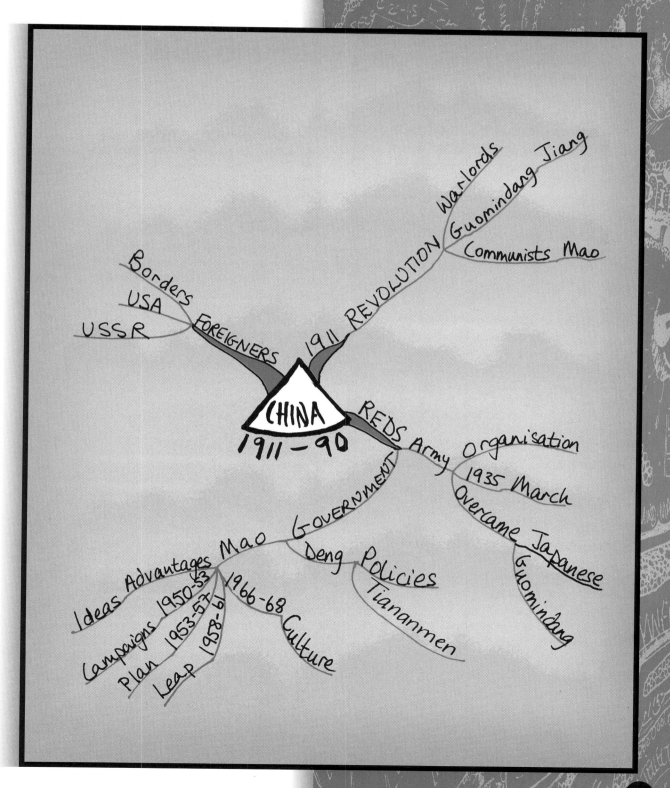

CHINA 1911–90

FOREIGNERS
- Borders
- USA
- USSR

1911 REVOLUTION
- Warlords
- Guomindang Jiang
- Communists Mao

REDS Army
- Organisation
- 1935 March
- Overcame Japanese
- Guomindang

GOVERNMENT
- Ideas Advantages Mao
- Deng Policies
- Tiananmen
- Campaigns 1950-53
- Plan 1953-57
- Leap 1958-61
- 1966-68 Culture

preview
What you need to know

- **Problems caused by the breakdown of government in China after 1911**

- **How the Communists grew in strength and took over the country**

- **How Mao ruled China**

- **The changes which Deng introduced**

- **How China has dealt with the rest of the world**

warning!

China is a vast country, containing a quarter of the world's population. Remember this whenever you read anything that deals with it as one unit. Remember, too, that the government has ruthlessly controlled the flow of information available both to Chinese citizens and to foreigners.

Note

It is difficult to write Chinese names using the Western alphabet. The Chinese themselves now use the so-called pinyin system. So does this book, sometimes adding older versions in brackets.

The 1911 Revolution

Until 1911 China was governed by emperors. But in 1911 there was a rebellion and Yuan Shikai became president. He died in 1916. The new central government was very weak. Local warlords seized power in their own areas and fought each other to extend their territories.

Source A

'China was shredded by warlord wars. The peasants and labourers paid for these feudal wars in grain levies and in exorbitant taxes, for armies have to be paid and fed, and only China's peasantry – 90 per cent of the population – could do it. Armies also need recruits and only the peasantry could supply them. In some areas men were press-ganged while working the fields. In Szechuan province, taxes were levied seventy years in advance.'

Han Suyin: *The Morning Deluge* (1972)

Source B

Execution in a Chinese street, 1927

Revolution timetable

1923 The Soviet government persuaded the Communists and the Guomindang to combine to suppress the warlords.

1925 Sun Yixian died. Jiang Jiehi took over as leader of the Guomindang.

1926 The combined forces took over most of northern China. Jiang, with the help of some warlords, decided to wipe out the Communists, and take complete control of the country.

1927 Mao, with fewer than 100 men, driven into the hills.

Opposition to the warlords

There were two organisations which, combined, were strong enough to take on the warlords.

★ **The Guomindang (Kuomintang) government**, headed by Sun Yixian (Sun Yat-sen), believed in democracy and socialism. Their army was commanded by Jiang Jiehi (Chiang Kai-Chek), who had trained as a soldier in Japan and the USSR.

★ **The Communist Party**, who wanted to set up a Communist government. Most of them thought the best way to do this was to win the support of the industrial workers and take over the cities. One of the founders of the party, Mao Ze Dong disagreed. He thought they ought to win over the peasants and control the countryside.

Specimen questions

1 Study Source A. Why did many people in China welcome the United Front?　[5 marks]

2 Look at Source B. It is a photograph taken in 1927. What does it show about conditions in Chinese towns at the time?　[5 marks]

Hints

Remember it is one photograph taken in one town.

check

that you understand the problems faced by China after 1911.

The Communists take over

Mao's army

Mao decided to recruit an army to defeat Jiang. He said: '*without a people's army the people have nothing .... Political power grows out of the barrel of a gun*'.

Source A

'*Reading, writing, arithmetic were taught by officers to their men. The men sat on the ground tracing characters and figures in the dirt, since there were no paper or pencils. But the most powerful educational method consisted of ... debate .... Not only were battles and campaigns discussed, but the individual conduct of any commander could be criticised.*'

Agnes Smedley: *Battle Hymn of China* (1944)

Source B

'He had a way of making even the enemy do what he wanted – he called it regaining the initiative. He would lead the enemy by the nose. He always did .... He walked with us. He never used the stretcher we had prepared for him; he gave it to the wounded.'

Red Army soldier speaking of Mao, quoted in Han Suyin: *The Morning Deluge* (1972)

Source C

'Speak politely; buy at fair prices: return what you borrow: pay for what you damage; replace all doors and return the straw on which you sleep: dig latrines away from houses and fill them in when you leave; do not molest women, do not ill treat captives.'

Mao's rules for his army, 1927–8

Source D

Specimen question

Using the information in the sources, explain why Mao's army became so powerful and popular.

[15 marks]

Hints

Why might people have wanted to join the army? Why was Mao a popular commander? Why was the army popular in the countryside?

check

that you understand how Mao organised his army.

The Long March

Jiang's army was much larger than the Red Army, and in 1934 he trapped the Red Army in Southern China. The Red Army broke out and marched to the North to establish a new base there.

Source A

Source B

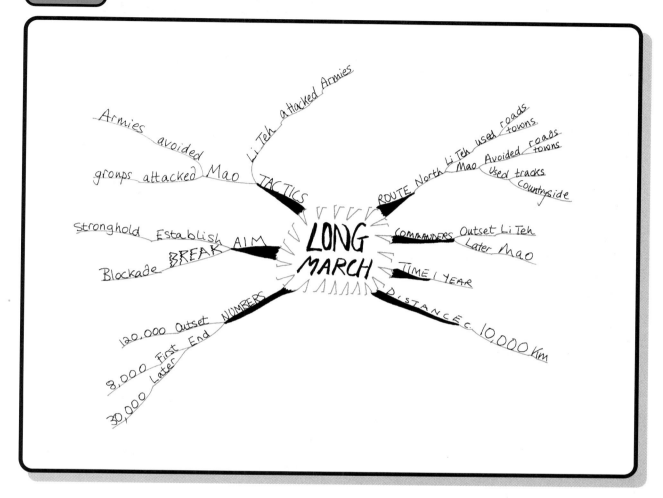

Long March mind map

TACTICS
- Armies avoided
- groups attacked Mao
- Li Teh attacked Armies

ROUTE North
- Li Teh used roads towns
- Mao Avoided roads towns
- Used tracks countryside

COMMANDERS Outset Li Teh Later Mao

TIME 1 YEAR

DISTANCE c. 10,000 Km

AIM Establish
- stronghold
BREAK
- Blockade

NUMBERS
- 120,000 Outset
- 8,000 First End
- 30,000 Later

Specimen questions

1. Study the sources. Why did the Red Army take such a roundabout route? **[3 marks]**

2. The Long March added greatly to Mao's prestige. Why was that? **[10 marks]**

Hint

Use your own knowledge as well as the sources to answer this question.

The war against Japan

In 1931 the Japanese had taken over Manchuria. By 1936 they were pushing further south. Jiang and Mao agreed to co-operate to drive them out. Mao's army fought in the north, Jiang's in the centre and south. Jiang fought pitched battles and usually lost. Mao did not.

Source A

'We must spread a guerrilla war all over the large areas occupied by the enemy, converting the enemy's rear into his front, and forcing him to fight ceaselessly throughout his occupied areas.'

Mao: Message to his army

Source B

'The enemy attacks, we retreat;
The enemy camps, we harass;
The enemy tires, we attack
The enemy retreats, we pursue.'

Poem taught to Mao's army

Source C

'The Communist government and armies are the
first in modern China to have positive and
widespread popular support .... because they are
genuinely of the people.'

John Paton Davies: Official report to the US
government (1944)

Japanese surrender

Gradually Mao drove the Japanese from the
countryside. By 1945, when the Japanese
surrendered, his army numbered 900,000 regulars
and about 2 million militia. It controlled about
100 million people.

Specimen questions

1 Why would the Japanese army find it
difficult to combat Mao's forces?   [4 marks]

2 Explain why, in 1945, many Chinese people
supported Communism.   [10 marks]

Hints

Associate it with: consideration for the poor,
honesty, patriotism, success, efficiency?

Remember to give examples.

The defeat of Jiang

After the defeat of the Japanese in 1945 Jiang,
who had been supported and equipped by the
USA, wanted to take over the whole of China. Mao
refused, in spite of the fact that Jiang's army was
five times as large as his. A new civil war broke
out. By 1949 it was over. Jiang lost, and fled to
Taiwan, where he set up his government.

check

that you understand how and why Mao was able
to take over the whole of China.

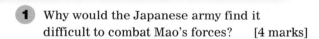

China under Mao

When Mao took over China he had a number of
advantages (*see* Mind Map on page 141).

He governed China through a council or
committee, of which he was chairman. The day-to-
day administration was controlled by the Prime
Minister, Zhou Enlai.

Mao seemed to trust the Chinese people.

Source A

'More people mean a greater ferment of ideas, more
enthusiasm and more energy. Never before have the
masses of the people been so inspired, so militant
and so daring as at present.'

Mao: *Introducing a Co-operative* (1958)

Source B

'Do not be afraid to make trouble. The more trouble
you make and the longer you make it the better.
Confusion and trouble always make an impact.
They can clear things up.'

Mao: *Advice to Party Members* (1949)

Specimen question

Why might Zhou Enlai have disagreed with Mao's views? Explain your answer.   [6 marks]

Hints

What was Zhou's job? Would more people, a 'ferment of ideas' and a lot of troublemakers make it easier or more difficult?

The early years 1950–3

Mao launched a series of campaigns to root out various 'evils' in Chinese life (*see* diagram below).

Specimen questions

1 Who would benefit from Mao's campaigns?
                                                [3 marks]

2 Who would enforce them?   [3 marks]

Hint

Use your own knowledge to answer these two questions.

The Five Year Plan 1953–7

As a rule China barely grew enough to feed its people and in bad years many starved. Industrial production was very low. Mao wanted to increase food production. He also wanted to make China into a great industrial power. The Five Year Plan was intended to achieve this. The Mind Map on page 142 will remind you of its main features.

Notes

Mao thought that collective farms would be big enough to afford machinery, fertilisers, etc. But the peasants disliked them. They wanted to own their own land. (Compare USSR.)

1950 'Three Mountains' against Feudalism, Capitalism and Imperialism.

1951 against counter-revolutionary landowners and capitalists. 250,000 executed.

Mao's campaigns

1952 'Three Antis' against corruption.

1953 'Five Antis' against profiteers.

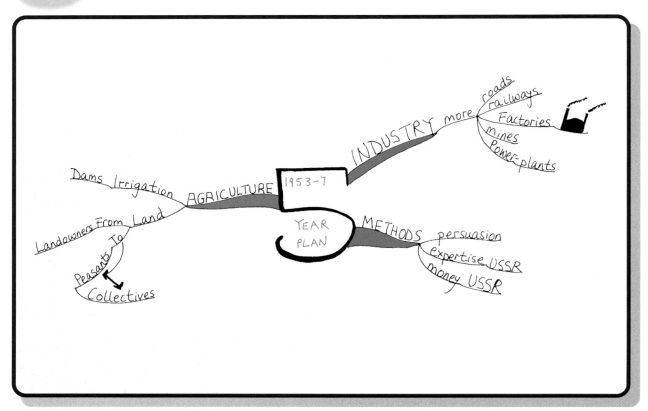

The mind map shows:

- **5 YEAR PLAN 1953-7** (central node)
- **INDUSTRY** more: roads, railways, Factories, mines, Power-plants
- **AGRICULTURE**: Dams, Irrigation, Landowners From Land To Peasants, Collectives
- **METHODS**: persuasion, expertise USSR, money USSR

Source A

Production table			
(million tonnes)	1952	1957	
		planned	actual
Coal	63.5	113	124
Iron	1.9	4.7	5.86
Steel	1.35	4.12	5.24
Oil	0.44	2.0	1.42
Cement	2.6	6.0	4.65
Power (billion kW)	7.26	15.9	19.1

Source B

'*Beijing was vivid … optimistic … Life had vastly improved.*'

Alan Waddington: *Breakfast with Mao* (1986)
(Waddington was an English writer living in China in the 1950s)

Specimen question

Study Source A. Are the figures quoted in it likely to be reliable? Explain your answer.   [4 marks]

Hints

What do the figures show about the success of the Five Year Plan? Who compiled them? Were they likely to be biased? In any case would it have been possible to get accurate figures from such a vast country?

Specimen question

Is Source B good evidence of the success of the Five Year Plan? Explain your answer.   [4 marks]

Hints

Might Waddington have been biased? Were conditions in Beijing necessarily typical of other parts of China?

The Great Leap Forward (1958–61)

Mao was not satisfied by the results of the Five Year Plan. He thought the people were hampered by officials. So he asked the people to tell him what they thought. He got a flood of complaints about collectivisation and high taxes, but no ideas which appealed to him. So he organised his Great Leap Forward, based on dividing the country into Communes. (*See* Mind Map.)

Source A

'In this way industry, agriculture, commerce, education and military affairs can be combined thus making the task of leadership easier.'

Mao: Speech, 1958

Source B

A propaganda woodcut publicising the Great Leap Forward

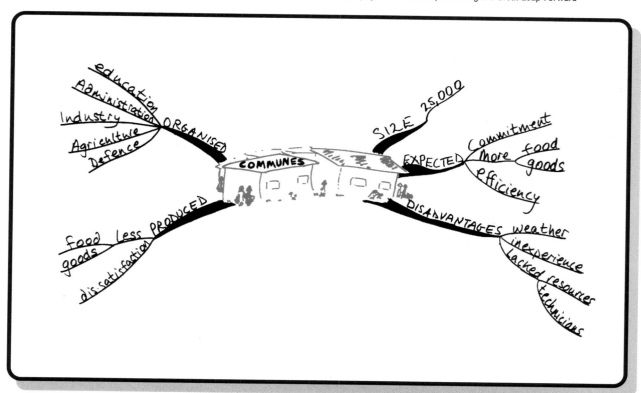

Source C

'There was no food to eat in the village. The peasants were eating the leaves of trees, boiling leaves in water, mixing them with a little cornflour to make the leaves stick together.'

Chinese Scholar quoted in Anne Thurston: *Enemies of the People* (1988)

Source D

Production table			
	1957	1960	
Grain	185	150	(million tonnes)
Cattle	50	42	(million head)
Sheep	52	50	
Pigs	145	82	

Study the Mind Map and Source A. Check that you understand Mao's aims.

Specimen questions

1 Study Sources B, C and D. Why might peasants have felt tricked and betrayed by the results of the Great Leap Forward?
[4 marks]

2 Study Sources C and D. Do the two sources give the same impression of the results of the Great Leap? If not, how can you account for the difference? [10 marks]

Hints

Look at Source D. Does it give the impression of (a) slight or (b) serious shortages? Ask the same question of Source C. To account for the differences, look at the hints for the questions on the Five Year Plan (pages 142–3). Remember to give examples taken from the sources to back up what you say.

check

that you understand the aims and results of the Great Leap Forward.

New policies

After the Great Leap Forward Mao lost some of his power. Prime Minister Zhou Enlai, President Liu Shaoqi and the Communist Party General Secretary Deng Xiaoping introduced new policies.

Encouraged people to set up their own businesses.

Gave bonuses for increased output.

Deng, Liu and Zhou's new policies

Grouped factories together and sent in technicians.

Gave peasants their own plots of land.

The Cultural Revolution

Mao hated the new reforms. He thought they were more like capitalism than communism. He feared that when he died the reformers would take over. So he decided to break them.

Mao knew he could rely on the army, and he was also supported by many students. He organised them into gangs of Red Guards, gave them copies of the *Little Red Book of Quotations from Chairman Mao Zedong* and told them to go out and rid the country of the 'Four Olds' – Old ideas, Old culture, Old customs and Old ways of life.

Source A

'[We vow to] apply sentence by sentence each of Chairman Mao's orders, even if we do not at first understand them.'

Oath taken by Red Guards

'Criticise … all the representatives of the bourgeoisie [middle classes] who have infiltrated the party, the government, the army and the cultural world.'

Party instruction to students, 16 May 1966

Source C

'The leftists ordered … criticism sessions in the courtyards of the houses of Liu and of Deng Xiaoping …. Liu and [his wife] were struck and kicked and made to sit in unbearably uncomfortable positions …. The session lasted over two hours. Liu's face was bruised and swollen.'

Beijing Workers' Daily (1980)
(Note: Liu and Deng were both disgraced. Liu disappeared and died. Deng had to work as a labourer for several years.)

Source D

'I saw rows of teachers … with black ink poured over their heads and faces …. They all wore dunces' caps …. Hanging from their necks were buckets filled with rocks.'

Ken Ling: *Red Guard: From Schoolboy to Little General* (1972)

Source E

'Red Guards … have caused work stoppages in the factories and the countryside by persuading workers and peasants that it is more important to intervene elsewhere than to work.'

Beijing Revolutionary Committee (1967)

Specimen questions

1 Who were the Red Guards? [4 marks]

2 What justification did they think they had for attacking **(a)** the teachers; **(b)** President Liu and Deng? [5 marks]

Hint

Look at Sources A and B.

Specimen question

What evidence is there in the sources that the Red Guards disrupted

(a) The government,

(b) Industry and agriculture,

(c) The educational system? [6 marks]

Hint

Beware! How general is the evidence in the sources?

The results of the Cultural Revolution

The Mind Map on page 146 will remind you of the results of the Cultural Revolution. Even Mao was alarmed. He had to use the army to disband the Red Guards. By the end of 1968 order had been restored.

check

that you understand the aims and results of the Cultural Revolution.

Mao's last years 1968–76

After 1968 Mao relied on Zhou Enlai and, after he had been reinstated in 1973, Deng Xiaoping. They thought that China needed a few years' peace and stability to recover from the Cultural Revolution. Mao's wife, Jiang Qing and several other left-wing communists did not agree. They wanted further reforms and tried to discredit Zhou and Deng. In 1976 Zhou and Mao both died. Jiang and three of her supporters – The Gang of Four – were arrested and imprisoned. By the middle of 1977 Deng had taken complete control.

check

your opinion of Mao. What were his strengths and his weaknesses?

China under Deng 1977–90

Deng's style of government

As a result of the policies below, production increased. Farmers and businessmen made money.

Farmers had to produce a quota for the community and kept the rest.

He increased the output of consumer goods.

He tried to limit the size of Chinese families.

Deng's policies

He insisted that Communist Party rule continued.

He encouraged foreigners to visit China and invest their money.

Factories had to produce a quota. Workers earned bonuses for extra.

He replaced elderly officials by young people.

Source A

'The main job of socialism is to increase production, steadily improve the life of the people and keep making society richer.'

Deng Xiaoping: Speech, 1986

Source B

'The colour of the cat does not matter so long as it catches the mouse.'

Deng Xiaoping: Saying

Source C

'In their heady pursuit of personal profit, many villagers ... [help] themselves to all kinds of public property .... There is more theft, more squabbling over land use and water.'

Lynn Pan: *The New Chinese Revolution* (1988)

Specimen question

Why did Deng introduce new policies after 1977? Explain your answer fully. [15 marks]

Hint

This question demands a lot of explanation. You need to explain how Mao's policies – particularly the Cultural Revolution – had failed, and how Deng hoped that his new, more practical policies (say what they were) would improve matters.

Specimen question

How could Deng's policies be blamed for the anti-social activities described by Lynn Pan (Source C)? [4 marks]

Tiananmen Square 1989

Deng Xiaoping kept tight control of the Chinese Communist Party.

In 1987 he dismissed the party chairman, Hu Yaobang (b. 1915) because he wanted more reforms than Deng thought right.

In 1988 Deng abolished price controls. Prices rose. There were riots. Deng reinstated controls.

In 1989 Hu Yaobang died, and a huge number of students gathered in Tiananmen Square in Beijing to mourn him and demand democratic reforms. The students and their supporters occupied the square for several weeks, in spite of being ordered to disperse. In the end armed troops with tanks cleared the square and the surrounding streets, killing hundreds of demonstrators. Later, thousands were arrested and imprisoned.

Source A

'The wrong man has died .... Those who should die still live. Those who should live have died.'

'China still has an emperor without an emperor's title, a senile and fatuous autocrat .... Down with autocracy .... Rule by old men must end.'

Student slogans in Tiananmen Square

Source B

'A serious counter-revolutionary rebellion has broken out in the capital. The People's Liberation Army has been restrained for some days. However the counter-revolutionary rebellion must now be resolutely counter-attacked.'

Army proclamation in Tiananmen Square, 2 a.m. June 4 1989

Source C

'As bodies crumpled to the ground, the crowd behind them scattered .... The army delivered a finale of machine gun fire from armoured troop carriers. Then, for a moment the avenue was still: a hundred yard length of corpses, abandoned bicycles and prone, terrified survivors. That first drama would repeat itself many times during the day.'

Fathers and Higgins: *Tiananmen* (1989)
(The authors were British journalists in Beijing in 1989)

History Revision Guide

8

Specimen question

Why did the Chinese government decide to crush the demonstrators in Tiananmen Square? Explain your answer fully. [10 marks]

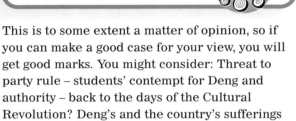

Hint

This is to some extent a matter of opinion, so if you can make a good case for your view, you will get good marks. You might consider: Threat to party rule – students' contempt for Deng and authority – back to the days of the Cultural Revolution? Deng's and the country's sufferings in the Cultural Revolution remembered? Remember to back up what you say by examples from the sources and your own knowledge.

Specimen question

Why did the government hesitate so long before sending the troops in? [5 marks]

Hint

Remember Mao's quote in 1949: '*Do not be afraid to make trouble.*' Should they use the army to crush people 'making trouble'? Remember the number of foreign correspondents in Beijing. What effect would using the army have on public opinion abroad? Refer to Source C? Why did foreign opinion matter?

check

that you understand what Deng was trying to do and why he crushed the students in Tiananmen Square.

China and the outside world 1949–90

Chinese borders

The Chinese revolutionary government claims all the territory traditionally ruled by the emperors.

The table shows the main areas lost by China, and what Communist governments have done to resolve the problems.

Mongolia	Taken by Russia in 1911. Became independent Mongolian People's republic in 1924.	Sino–Soviet Treaty guaranteed independence in 1950. Border with China agreed in 1987.
Macao	Seized by Portugal in 1511.	Chinese take over in 1999.
Hong Kong	Taken over by Britain 1841–98.	Chinese take over in 1997. Capitalist system guaranteed for 50 years.
Tibet	Became independent of China under British influence in 1911.	China reoccupied Tibet in 1950.
Taiwan	Japan occupied it in 1895. Jiang Jiehi (Chiang Kai-Chek) took over in 1945.	Chinese have offered the same terms as for Hong Kong. No agreement.

Wars on China's borders

Korea	**1950**	Invaded Korea when General Mac Arthur threatened to cross the Yalu River into China.
India	**1962**	Accused India of supporting a rebellion in Tibet. Invaded India, defeated Indian forces and then withdrew.
USSR	**1969**	Following various border disputes, Chinese and USSR troops clashed on the Ussuri River.

Specimen question

Have the Chinese Communists been aggressive towards their neighbours? Explain your answer. [10 marks]

Hint

What does 'aggressive' mean? Could the Chinese claim they were only trying to get back and protect their own? How might that seem to their neighbours? Remember to give examples to illustrate your general points.

China and the USSR

At first China was on good terms with the USSR, and relied on Russian help to build up industry and agriculture.

But Mao distrusted the Russians. He disagreed with their policy of peaceful co-existence with the West, and disapproved of the invasion of Czechoslovakia. So he openly criticised the Soviet government. In addition there were frequent border disputes, so relations between the two countries deteriorated.

China and the USA

After the Second World War the US government still recognised Jiang Jiehi as rightful ruler of China, even though he had been driven out to Taiwan. Mao feared that the USA wanted to overthrow the Communist government. He thought there would probably be a nuclear war between East and West. He invaded Korea when American troops threatened the Chinese frontier in 1950 and helped Communist forces in Vietnam to fight against the USA.

In 1971 President Nixon agreed to recognise the Communists as rightful rulers of China, and in 1972 he visited Beijing. Mao said it was '*a tactical alliance with a secondary enemy to defeat a primary one [the USSR].*'

Specimen question

What would you expect the following people to think of Nixon's visit to Beijing:

(a) A member of Jiang Jiehi's government on Taiwan,

(b) A Communist who supported the USSR,

(c) A US businessman who wanted to trade with China?

Explain your answers. [10 marks]

that you understand China's attitude to the rest of the world.

Index